**FOR
REFERENCE ONLY**

1958 Chrysler 300D Convertible

AUTOMOBILES
of the CHROME AGE
1946-1960

MICHAEL FURMAN

Harry N. Abrams, Inc., Publishers

A TEHABI BOOK

1954 Plymouth Belmont

For my parents

Fin Detail
1948 Cadillac 6207 Club Coupé

POSTWAR

1947 Tatra T87

1947 Cisitalia 202SM "Nuvolari Spyder"

1947 Cisitalia 202SM "Nuvolari Spyder"

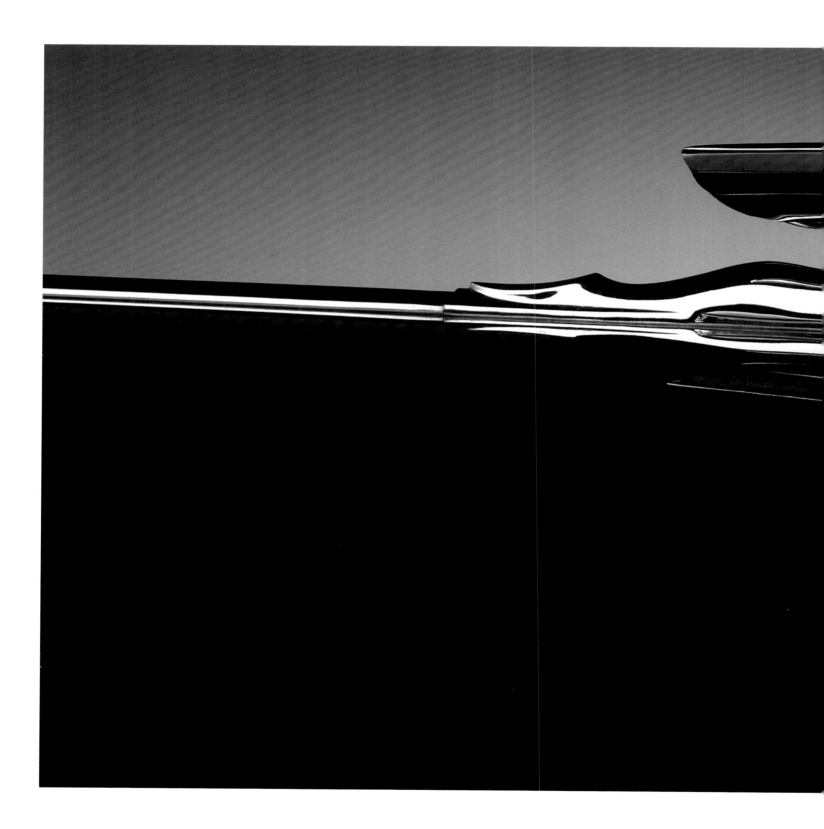

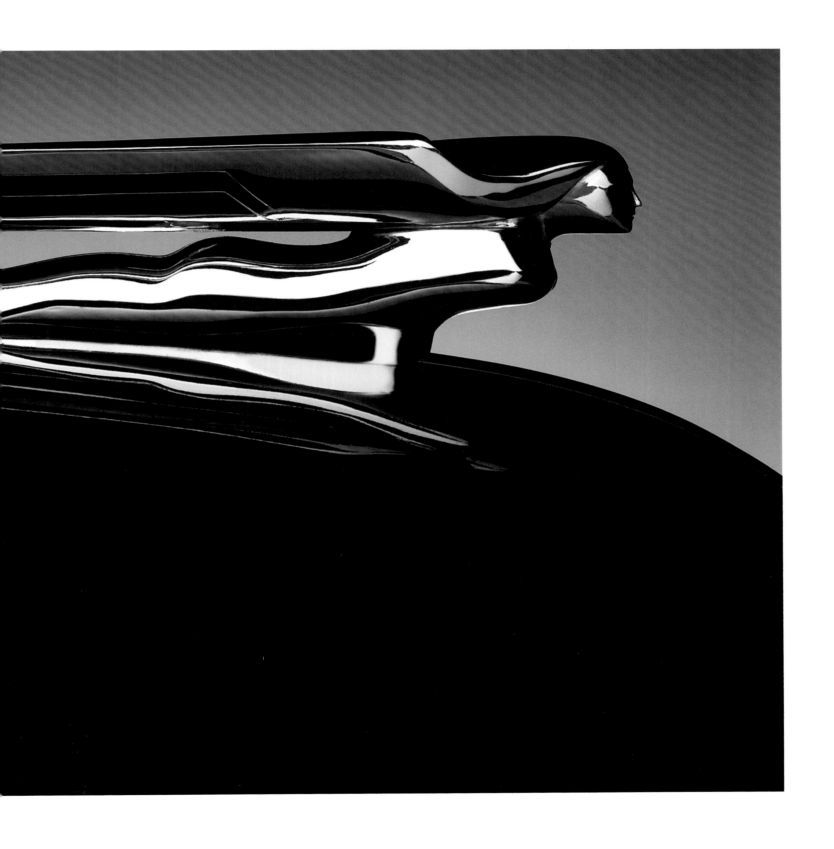

Hood Ornament
1947 Nash Ambassador Suburban

1947 Nash Ambassador Suburban

1947 Nash Ambassador Suburban

Door Handles
1947 Nash Ambassador Suburban

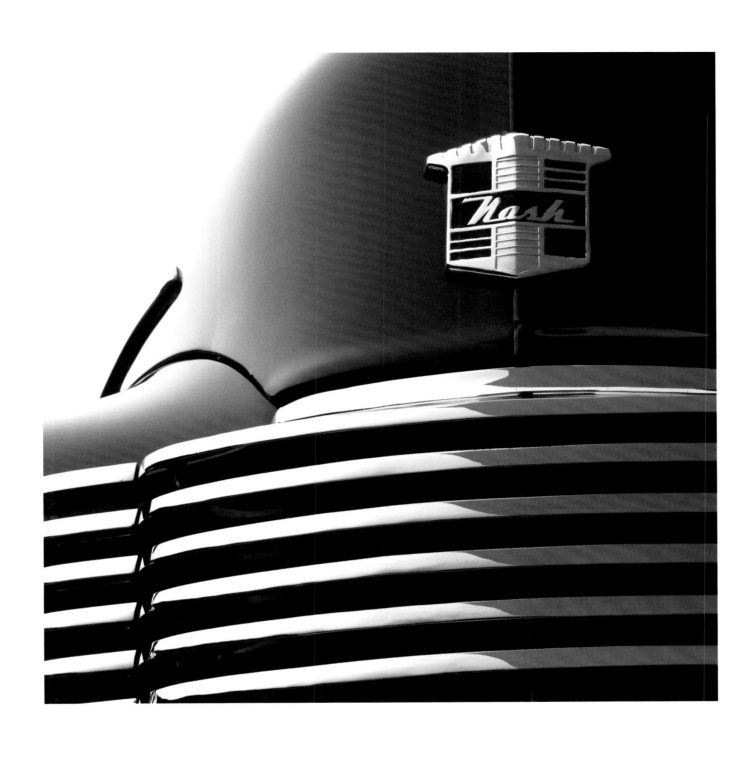

Grille Detail
1947 Nash Ambassador Suburban

1947 Ford Woody Wagon DeLuxe

1948 Mercury Convertible

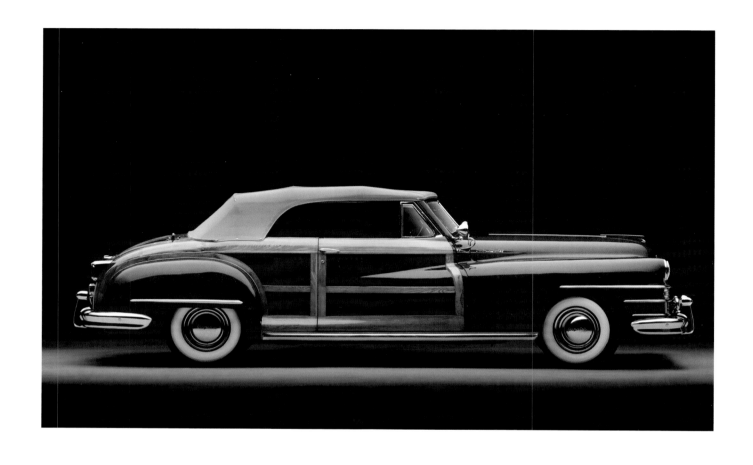

1948 Chrysler Town & Country Convertible

1950 Volkswagen

Rear Window Detail
1950 Volkswagen

1947 Cadillac 6207 Club Coupé

1948 Cadillac 6207 Club Coupé

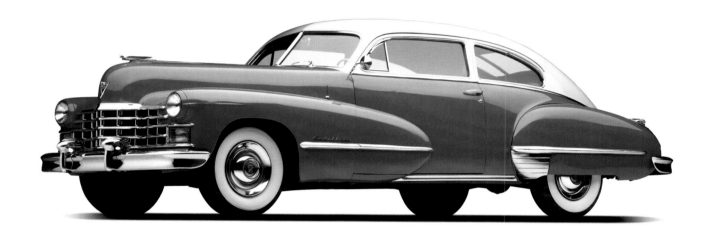

1947 Cadillac 6207 Club Coupé

1948 Cadillac 6207 Club Coupé

1948 Tucker

1949 Buick Roadmaster Convertible

1949 Buick Roadmaster Convertible

Window Crank
1949 Buick Roadmaster Convertible

Trunk Handle
1949 Buick Roadmaster Convertible

Taillight Detail
1949 Buick Roadmaster Convertible

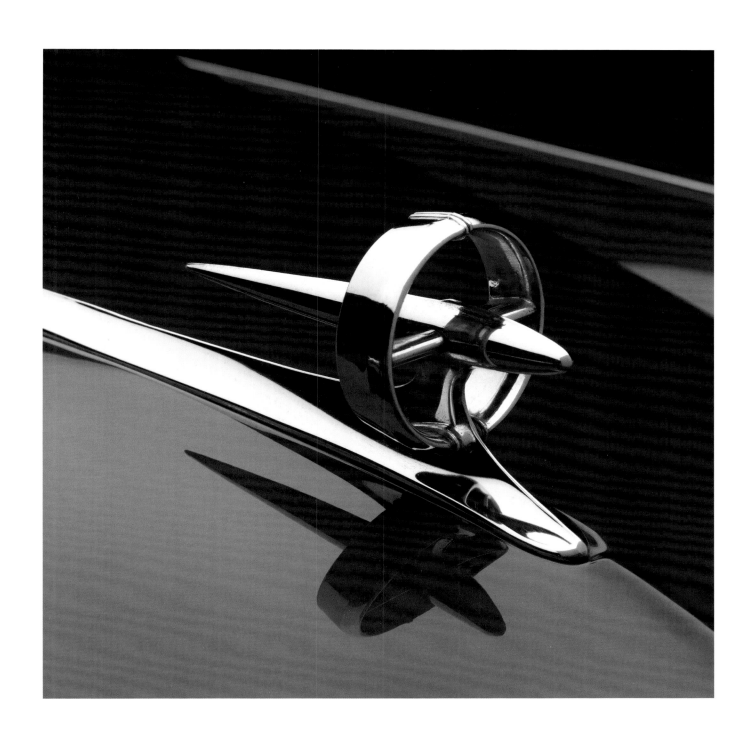

Hood Ornament
1949 Buick Roadmaster Convertible

Portholes
1949 Buick Roadmaster Convertible

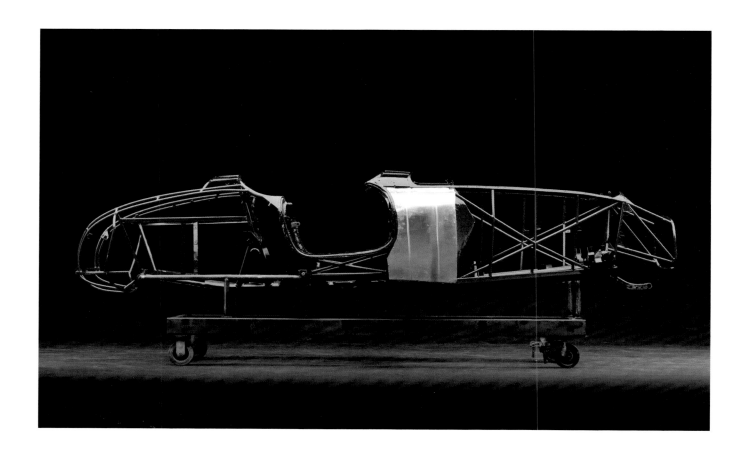

Frame
1949 Ferrari 166MM "Barchetta"

Body Panels
1949 Ferrari 166MM "Barchetta"

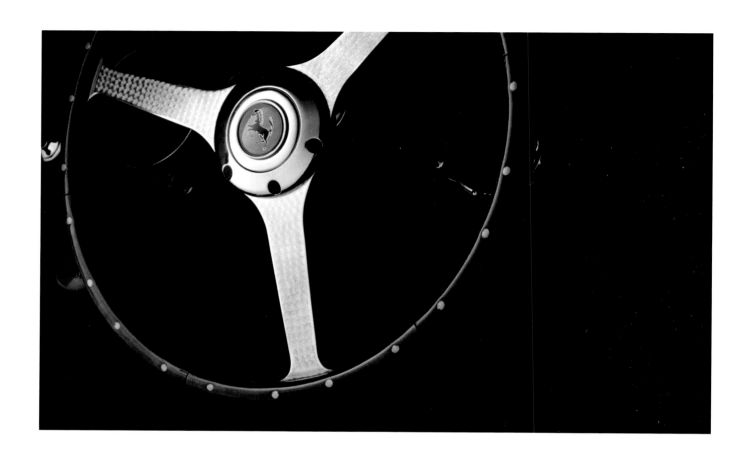

Steering Wheel Detail
1949 Ferrari 166MM "Barchetta"

Grille and Headlight Detail
1952 Jaguar XK120 Fixed Head Coupé

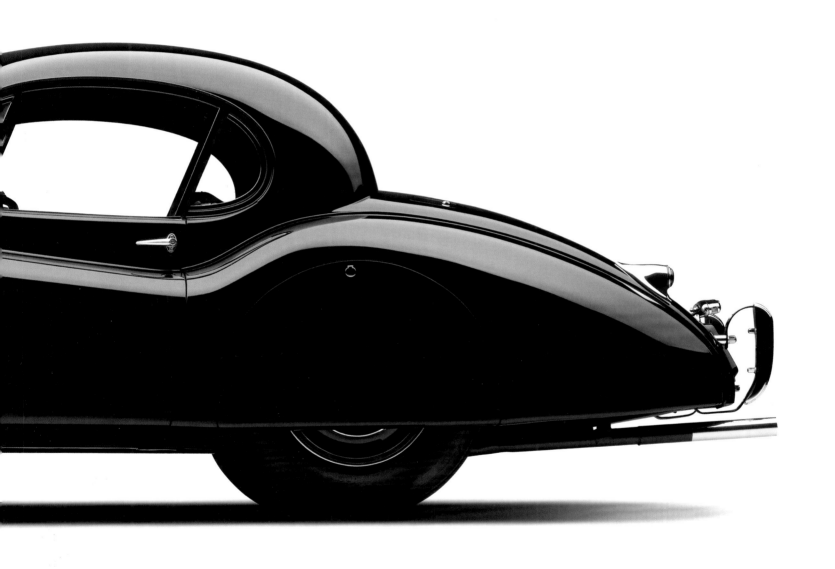

1952 Jaguar XK120 Fixed Head Coupé

1952 Jaguar XK120 Open Two-Seater

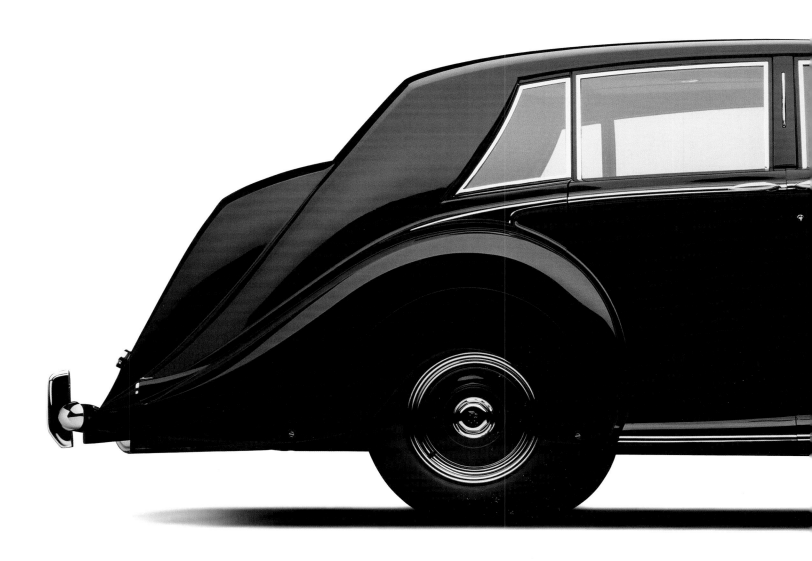

1950 Rolls-Royce Silver Wraith

by Hooper

THE EARLY 1950s

1951 Buick LeSabre

Hood Ornament
1950 Packard Custom Eight Convertible

Grille Detail
1952 Studebaker Commander Convertible

1950 Packard Custom Eight Convertible

1952 Studebaker Commander Convertible

1951 Hudson Hornet

1951 Hudson Hornet

1953 Bentley R-Type Continental

by H. J. Mulliner

1951 Hudson Hornet

1953 Bentley R-Type Continental

by H. J. Mulliner

Hood Badge
1952 Cunningham C-4RK

Hood Badge
1956 Dual Ghia Convertible Coupé

1953 Ferarri 375MM

80

1953 Ferarri 375MM

1954 Frazer Nash LeMans Coupé

1953 Bristol 401

1953 Nash Healey

1953 Chevrolet Corvette

1953 Nash Healey

1953 Chevrolet Corvette

Hood Badge
1953 Nash Healey

1953 Alfa Romeo 1900C SS

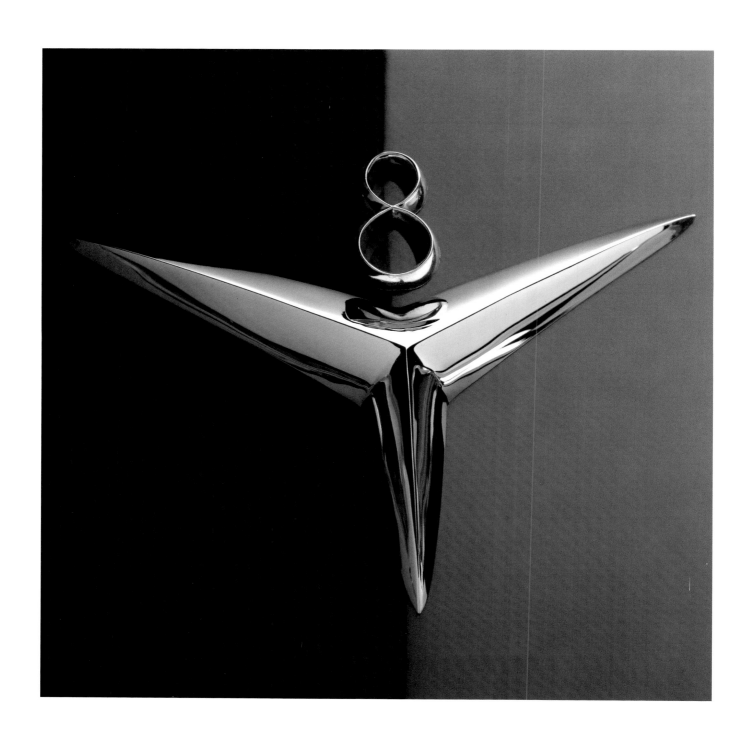

Hood Badge
1953 Studebaker Commander Starliner

Hood Badge
1954 Frazer Nash LeMans Coupé

1955 Triumph TR2

1960 Triumph TR3A

1955 Triumph TR2

1951 Rolls-Royce Silver Dawn

1953 Mercedes-Benz 300S Cabriolet

1953 Studebaker Commander Starliner

1953 Studebaker Commander Starliner

1953 Cadillac Eldorado Convertible

1953 Buick Skylark

1953 Buick Skylark

1954 Dodge Firearrow

1954 Buick Skylark

1955 Porsche 550 Spyder

1954 Buick Skylark

Fin Detail
1954 Buick Skylark

Side Badge
1954 Buick Skylark

1954 Plymouth Belmont

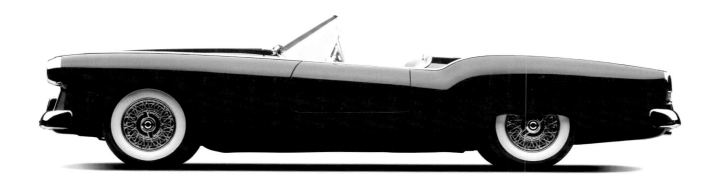

1954 Plymouth Belmont

1956 Dual Ghia Convertible Coupé

1955 Ford Thunderbird

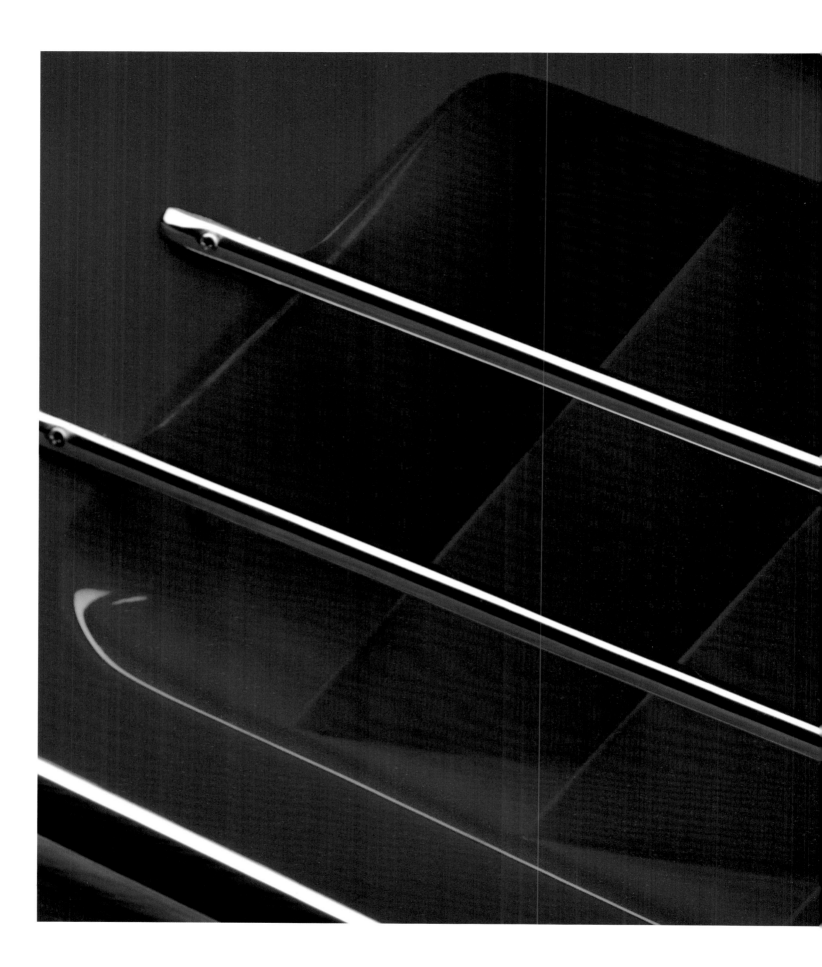

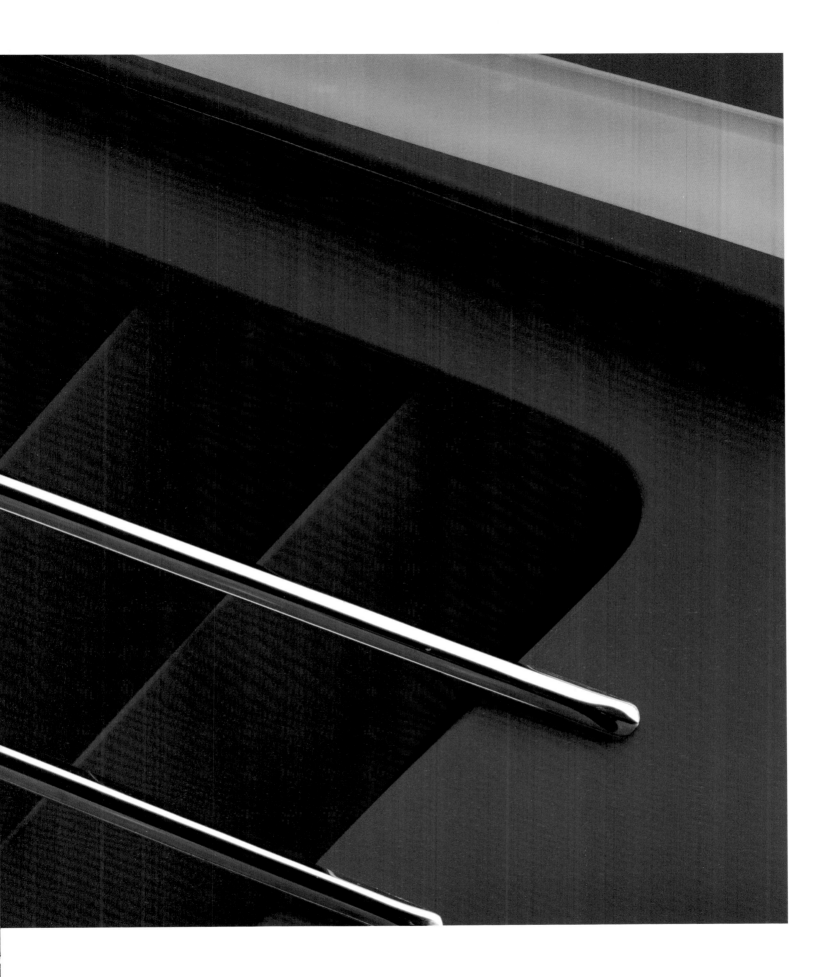

Side Vents
1956 Mercedes-Benz 300SL Coupé

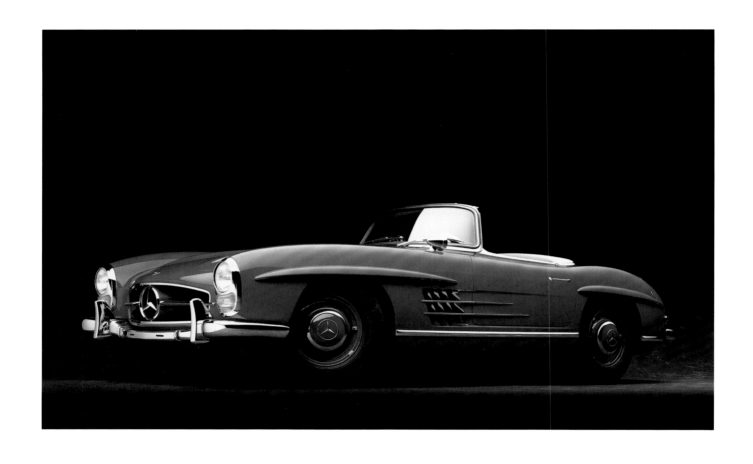

1958 Mercedes-Benz 300SL Roadster

1956 Mercedes-Benz 300SL Coupé

Grille Detail
1955 Mercedes-Benz 300SL Alloy Coupé

Seat Detail
1955 Mercedes-Benz 300SL Alloy Coupé

1956 Jaguar 3.4 Saloon

1955 Aston Martin DB2/4 Drop Head Coupé

1959 Aston Martin DB2/4 MkIII

1956 Austin-Healey 100M LeMans

1956 Nash Metropolitan

1953 Bristol 401

1956 BMW Isetta 300

Badge
1953 Bristol 401

Tailgate Detail
1955 Chevrolet Nomad

1955 Chevrolet Nomad

Hood Ornament
1956 Chevrolet Two-Ten Sport Coupé

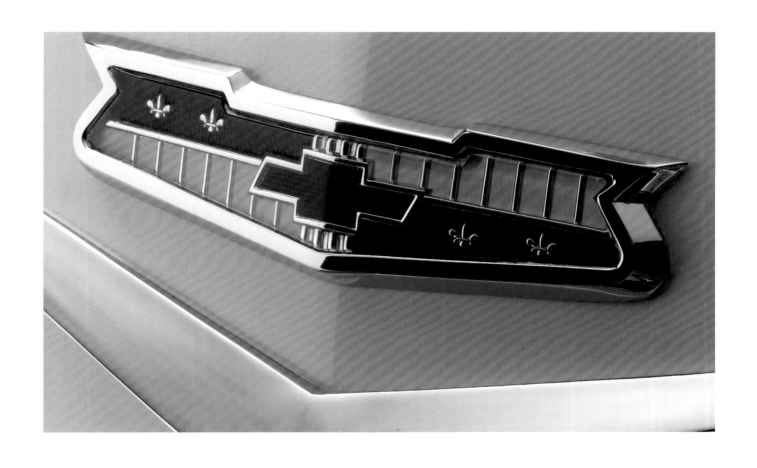

Hood Badge
1956 Chevrolet Two-Ten Sport Coupé

1956 Chevrolet Two-Ten Sport Coupé

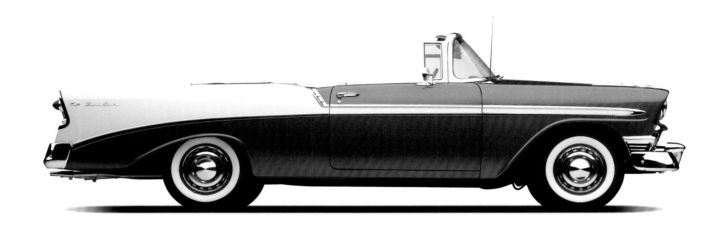

1956 Chevrolet Bel Air Convertible

1956 Chevrolet Two-Ten Sport Coupé

Dash Clock
1956 Chevrolet Bel Air Convertible

Wheel Cover Detail
1956 Chevrolet Bel Air Convertible

1955 Chrysler Imperial

1955 Chrysler Imperial

1955 Chrysler Imperial

Console Detail
1955 Chrysler Imperial

Rear Badge
1955 Chrysler Imperial

1956 De Soto Adventurer

1955 Chrysler Imperial

Hood Badge
1955 Chrysler Imperial

Taillight
1955 Chrysler Imperial

Wheel Cover Detail
1956 De Soto Adventurer

Taillight Detail
1956 De Soto Adventurer

1956 Lincoln Premiere

1956 Lincoln Premiere

1956 Ford Crown Victoria Skyliner

1956 Ford Crown Victoria Skyliner

Side Badge
1956 Ford Crown Victoria Skyliner

Hood Badge
1956 Ford Crown Victoria Skyliner

Continental Kit Detail
1956 Ford Thunderbird

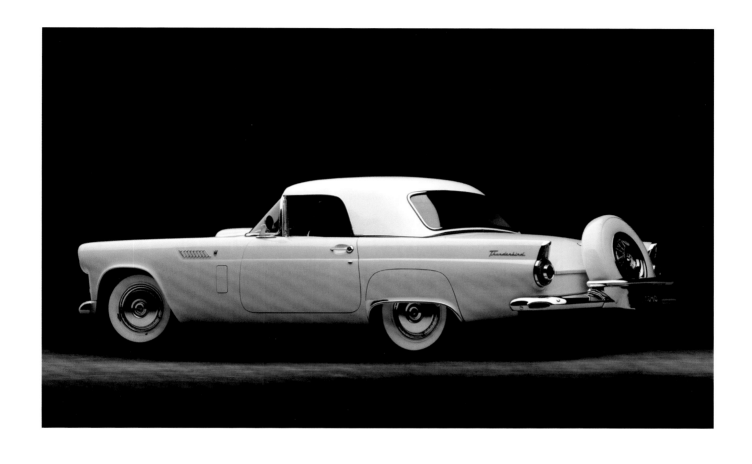

1956 Ford Thunderbird

1956 Continental Mk II

1956 Continental Mk II

Taillight Detail
1956 Continental Mk II

1956 Continental Mk II

THE LATE 1950s

1957 Chrysler 300C

1958 Chrysler 300D Convertible

1957 Ford Fairlane 500 Skyliner

1959 De Soto Adventurer Convertible

1957 Chevrolet Bel Air Convertible

1957 Chevrolet Bel Air Convertible

1957 Oldsmobile Super 88 Convertible

1957 Cadillac Eldorado Brougham

1957 Pontiac Star Chief Custom Safari Station Wagon

1957 Pontiac Star Chief Custom Safari Station Wagon

Hood Badge and Grille Detail
1957 Pontiac Star Chief Custom Safari Station Wagon

Hood Ornament
1957 Oldsmobile Super 88 Convertible

1958 Chevrolet Bel Air Impala Coupé

1958 Chevrolet Bel Air Impala Coupé

Decal
1958 Ferrari 250 Testa Rossa

Wheel Detail
1958 Ferrari 250 Testa Rossa

1958 Ferrari 250 Testa Rossa

1958 Porsche 718 RSK

1957 Lancia Aurelia

1956 Porsche 356A Carrera Speedster

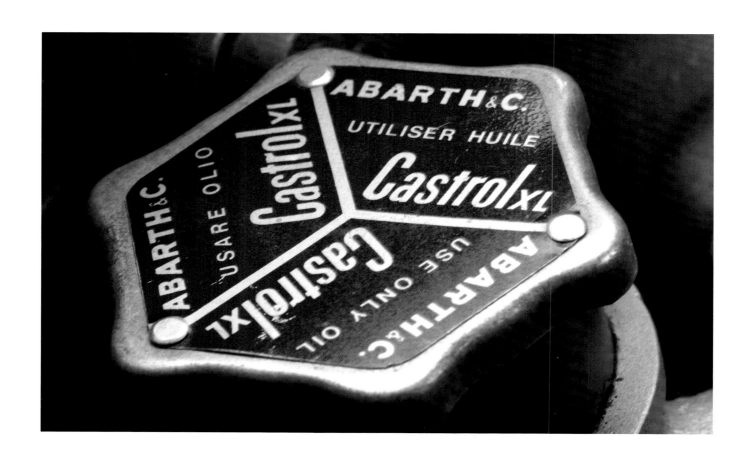

Oil Cap
1959 Fiat Abarth Record Monza Bialbero Zagato

Steering Wheel Detail
1957 Lancia Aurelia

1958 BMW 507

1958 MGA Roadster

1958 MGA Coupé

1957 O.S.C.A. S187

Cockpit Detail
1958 Ferrari 250 Testa Rossa

Gas Tank Detail
1957 O.S.C.A. S187

Headlight Detail
1960 Porsche 356 Carrera GT

Rear Deck Detail
1960 Porsche 356 Carrera GT

1959 Saab 750GT

1959 Fiat Abarth Record Monza Bialbero Zagato

1959 Chevrolet Impala Sport Coupé

Taillight Detail
1958 Chevrolet Bel Air Impala Coupé

Continental Kit Detail
1959 Chevrolet Impala Sport Coupé

Taillight Detail
1960 Pontiac Bonneville Convertible

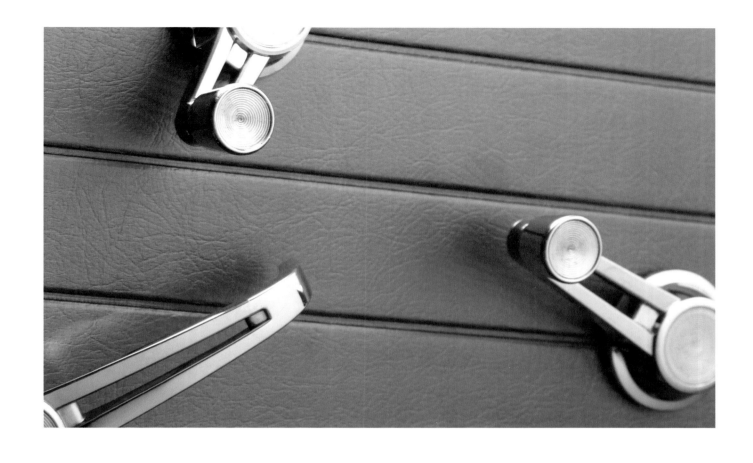

Interior Door Detail
1960 Pontiac Bonneville Convertible

1959 Chevrolet Impala Convertible

1957 Rolls-Royce Silver Cloud I

by H. J. Mulliner

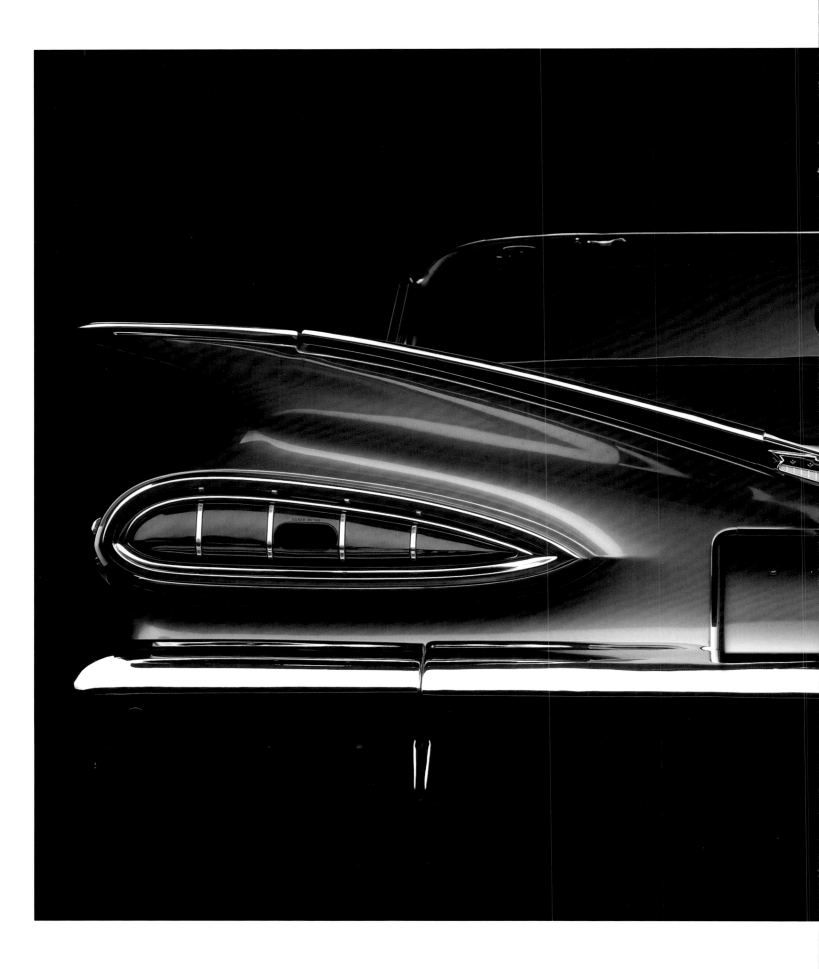

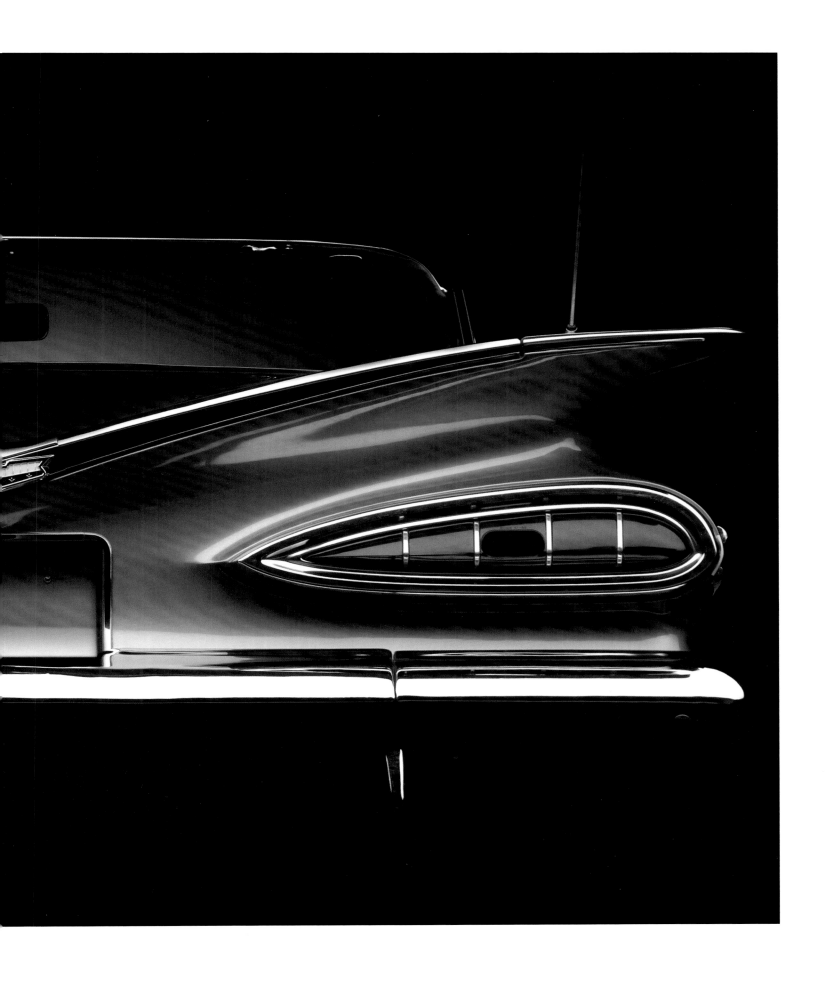

1959 Chevrolet Impala Convertible

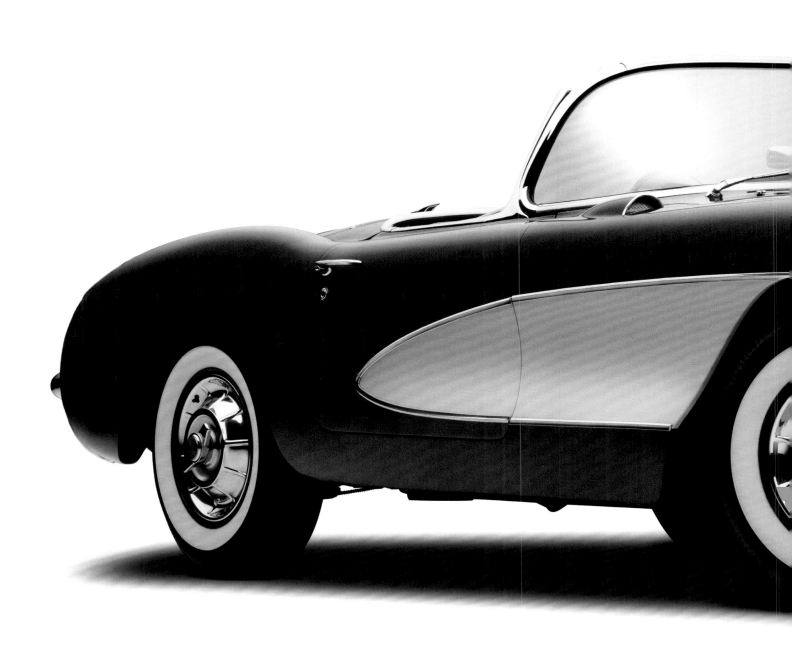

1957 Chevrolet Corvette

1960 Aston Martin DB4GT Zagato

1960 Aston Martin DB4GT Zagato

1960 Aston Martin DB4GT

1960 Chevrolet Corvette

Wheel Detail
1960 Aston Martin DB4GT

Grille Detail
1960 Aston Martin DB4GT

1960 Chevrolet Corvette

1959 Bentley S-1 Continental Sport Coupé
by Park Ward

1959 Firebird III

1959 Cadillac 60 Special Fleetwood

1959 Cadillac Series 62 Convertible

1959 Cadillac Eldorado Seville Hardtop

1959 Cadillac Eldorado Seville Hardtop

1959 Cadillac Eldorado Seville Hardtop

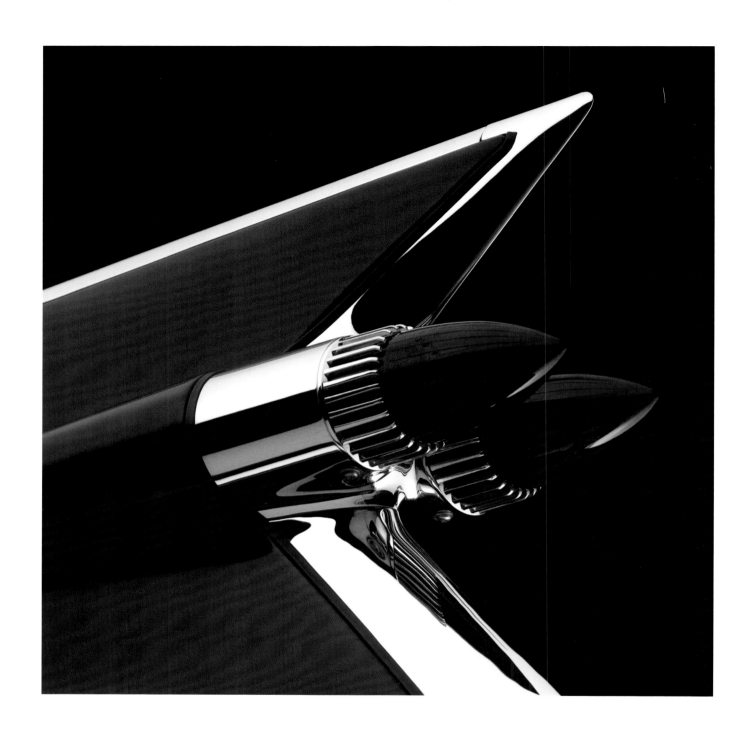

Taillight and Fin Detail
1959 Cadillac Eldorado Seville Hardtop

ALFA ROMEO
Italy

ASTON MARTIN
England

Alfa Romeo is one of the great automotive marques, with a storied racing heritage and a legacy of light and fast, limited production touring cars. It began when a small Milan firm, Anonima Lombarda Fabbrica Automobili (A.L.F.A.), was purchased by industrialist Nicola Romeo in 1915. Romeo's passion for racing and the work of the marque's famed engine designer, Vittorio Jano, led the company to a succession of victories at LeMans, the Mille Miglia, and numerous Grand Prix events in the 1930s.

1953 ALFA ROMEO 1900C SS

Throughout the war years, Alfa Romeo produced cars in very small numbers. By 1950, however, the firm's manufacturing evolved to larger scale fabrication on new assembly lines. Orazio Satta, who had joined Alfa in 1938, created the 4-cylinder 1900 series—an elegant coupé by Touring—and the Pininfarina cabriolet. Other, more exclusive custom bodies were also produced.
[page 89]

The first Aston Martin was produced in 1922 and immediately made its debut into the British racing scene, its name a combination of cofounder Lionel Martin's surname and Martin's favorite race, the Aston Clinton hill-climb. Though Martin and his business partner Robert Bamfort produced only a few cars, they achieved remarkable success at LeMans, the Ulster Tourist Trophy, and the Brooklands Double twelve-hour races. Over the next twenty years, however, the marque became equally well known for its financial troubles and continual changes in management. Finally in 1947, the financial dust settled when industrialist David Brown took control of the company. The Two-Litre was the new company's first offering. Then the following year, Brown purchased Lagonda, gaining access to the highly regarded twin-ohc 2580cc 6-cylinder engine designed by W. O. Bentley.

1955 ASTON MARTIN
DB2/4 DROP HEAD COUPÉ

The DB2 first appeared in April 1950. The aluminum two-seater coupé was designed in-house by Frank Feeley and made use of the 105 horsepower Lagonda engine. By the end of 1953, the DB2/4—which seated four—debuted with a 2922cc, 140 horsepower engine. Almost five hundred hatchbacks and seventy-five cabriolets were built during its two years of production.
[page 124]

1959 ASTON MARTIN
DB2/4 MKIII

The MkIII debuted as the final version of the venerable DB2. Unlike its predecessors, the MkIII was produced by Tickford Works of Newport Pagnell

—a coach building company purchased by David Brown in 1954. Feeley freshened the look using elements from the DB3 racecars, upgrading its performance with disc brakes and a 178 horsepower engine.
[page 125]

1960 ASTON MARTIN
DB4GT

The all-new DB4 was a larger car with a 3670cc twin-ohc aluminum engine designed by Tadek Marek. Production began in September 1958, and one year later, the GT debuted with a shortened wheelbase and a power increase to 302 horsepower at 6,000 rpm. The top speed was a heady 170 miles per hour. Carrozzeria Touring styled the DB4GT, using its *superleggera* technique of hand-formed aluminum panels over steel frame construction.
[pages 226, 228, 229]

1960 ASTON MARTIN
DB4GT ZAGATO

Zagato of Milan transformed the DB4GT into a lighter, more capable racecar. A mere nineteen of these ultralightweight cars were built, each one almost four hundred pounds lighter than the standard car. With softer, more flowing lines, the DB4GT Zagato has become the most treasured of the "David Brown Astons."
[pages 224, 225]

AUSTIN-HEALEY
England

BENTLEY
England

Donald Mitchell Healey hailed from Cornwall, England, and loved small sports cars. As a young man, he lent his name to a number of limited-production, high-quality cars such as the Nash-Healey and the Healey Silverstone. The Austin-Healey was the combination of Healey's chassis and body, powered by an Austin 2.6-litre, 4-cylinder engine. At the 1952 London Motor Show at the Earl's Court Exhibition Hall, Austin's chairman, Leonard Lord, agreed to the deal that would give this new company its name.

1956 AUSTIN-HEALEY
100M LEMANS

American servicemen returning from European duty had enjoyed driving British sports cars during their free time—particularly the MG-TC and

Jaguar XK120. Donald Healey saw there was a market niche for his Gerry Coker designed two-seater, so with Leonard Lord's backing, he introduced the 100 to the American market in 1953. Two years later, they took the higher performance 100M LeMans to the public. This model honored the marque's success in its debut at the 1953 LeMans twenty-four-hour race.

Eventually 90 percent of production went to export markets, helping to revitalize Britain's postwar economy. In 1973 Queen Elizabeth II recognized Healey's contribution to his country and named him Commander of the Order of the British Empire.
[pages 126–127]

Bentley was an independent company founded by W. O. Bentley in 1919. Despite racking up many successes on the track— including wins at LeMans from 1927 through 1930—the young firm struggled financially. In 1931 Bentley became a wholly owned subsidiary of Rolls-Royce, remaining with the firm until 2003.

Bentley's postwar cars borrowed heavily from Rolls-Royce, which still used prewar styling and mechanicals. The Bentley MkVI first appeared in early 1946, and although it resembled the Rolls-Royce Silver Wraith, it was usually delivered with a standard body. The two marques remained similar until the early 1980s, when they moved on to more distinctive styling.

1953 BENTLEY R-TYPE
CONTINENTAL
by H. J. Mulliner

At $18,000, the R-Type Continental was the most expensive and fastest four-passenger production car of its day. John Blatchley, the in-house stylist at Rolls-Royce, used aerodynamic studies performed in a wind tunnel to sculpt the aluminum fast-back body. This was a dramatic departure from the Rolls-Royce MkVI, and cemented the R-Type's reputation as one of the most beautiful cars of all time.

[pages 74, 76–77]

1959 BENTLEY S-1
CONTINENTAL SPORT
COUPÉ
by Park Ward

The S-Type Bentley replaced the R-Type in 1955. Other than the radiator shell, the car was identical to the Rolls-Royce Silver Cloud, with a standard body built by Pressed Steel and custom coachwork by either H. J. Mulliner or Park Ward. The two-door Continental, however, was available only in coupé or convertible styles.
[pages 232–233]

BMW traces its roots to airplane engine production in 1916, its logo a stylized propeller. Part of the German war effort, its factories in Munich were repeated targets during World War II.

The East German Eisenach plant began producing cars again in 1945, while the West German Munich facility resumed motorcycle production in 1948. The first car to be released from Munich was the 501, which debuted in 1951 using the engine and transmission of the prewar 326 model. The 501 continued BMW's tradition of building fine cars for the discriminating enthusiast rather than producing cheaper models for the masses. Unfortunately, this business strategy left BMW in significant financial trouble as it struggled to find wealthy buyers in postwar Germany. The company stayed afloat, however, fending off a takeover from Daimler-Benz in 1959 to remain an independent manufacturer.

1956 BMW ISETTA 300

Recognizing the need to produce in higher volumes, BMW licensed the three-wheeled "bubble car" from the Italian builder Iso. This tiny car, called the "Isetta," featured a steering column that moved aside when the single front-facing door was opened. Due to its small 245cc engine and single rear wheel, the Isetta was given motorcycle status—and consequently, lower road taxes. This made the car attractive to the common buyer.

[page 131]

1958 BMW 507

The beautiful 507 was BMW's glory car of the 1950s. Designed by Count Albrecht Goertz, just 252 of these aluminum-bodied, V-8 powered cars were built over five years. The car was designed to lead BMW to more financially secure footing, but it was expensive and faced fierce competition from the Mercedes-Benz 300SL. Even so, such luminaries as world racing champion John Surtees and Elvis Presley chose to own this handsome roadster.

[pages 200–201]

Like BMW, Bristol— founded in 1910—also traces its roots to aircraft manufacturing. After developing planes for the Royal Air Force in World War II, Bristol began making exclusive, high-quality cars with its excess production capability. As part of war reparations, Bristol was able to gain use of BMW's prewar 326 and 327 designs, and created the Bristol 400. The 400 resembled the BMW 327 with its split grille and flowing fenders. Later, Fritz Fiedler, designer of BMW's 328 engine, joined the firm and created the 1971cc, 85 horsepower engine for the 400 series. But it was the aircraft quality and limited production that defined Bristol's niche.

1953 BRISTOL 401

Arriving in 1948, the 401 was Bristol's first postwar design. Its construction incorporated *superleggera* techniques of shaping thin aluminum body panels over a small-tube steel frame. Aerodynamic testing resulted in an efficient, futuristic, teardrop shape. Just 650 coupés were made.

[pages 83, 130, 132]

The Buick Motor Company dates to 1903, when David Dunbar Buick built his first gasoline engine. The young company needed financial support, however, and was acquired by William C. Durant the following year. In quick succession, Durant acquired Oldsmobile, Cadillac, and Oakland to create General Motors Corporation. With its reputation for building reliable, quality vehicles, Buick proved popular. By 1923 the marque had produced one million cars, building two million more by the end of 1936. During the war years, Buick shifted to military production, building Pratt & Whitney aircraft engines, Hellcat tank destroyers, and other war material. In 1942 Harley Earl restyled the car, using design themes from his famous 1938 "Y-Job" show car. This progressive design was well received by the public and allowed Buick to return to passenger car production in October 1945 with minimal restyling or retooling.

1949 BUICK ROADMASTER
CONVERTIBLE

Buick introduced its first major postwar models in 1949. Harley Earl's fuselage design allowed for the front fenders to join the body with only minimal flaring for the rear fenders. A "bombsight" hood ornament topped the massive grille, while portholes on each side added to the Roadmaster's aggressive looks.

[pages 44, 45, 46, 47, 48, 49, 50–51]

1951 BUICK LESABRE

The LeSabre was the second concept car created by Harley Earl and his team from the Art & Colour Section of General Motors. It followed the "Y-Job" by thirteen years,

taking its predecessor's long, low, aerodynamic shape even further into the future. The F86 jet fighter served as inspiration for the car's large, center port on the hood, dramatic rear deck, and fins. The aluminum body was even stretched over a special steel frame that featured a hidden top that closed automatically when a device between the front seats sensed rain. An altimeter on the dash completed the aerodynamic feel.

[pages 64–65]

1953 BUICK SKYLARK

General Motors produced three exclusive convertibles—the Buick Skylark, Cadillac Eldorado, and Oldsmobile Fiesta—in 1953. Stylist Ned Nickles,

who worked on the 1949 Roadmaster, lowered the windshield and used Kelsey Hayes chrome wire wheels. Intended as luxury transportation for the wealthy, the $5,000 Skylark was beautiful but ultimately considered too expensive. It sold fewer than 1,700 cars.

[pages 101, 102]

1954 BUICK SKYLARK

In 1954 Buick shortened the wheelbase of the Skylark and lowered the price by more than $500. The company also mounted chrome fins above the taillight housings, making the rear of the car its most distinctive view. These changes weren't enough to save the car, though. The Skylark sold only half the number of cars it did the previous year, and it was discontinued in 1955.

[pages 104–105, 107, 108, 109]

In 1902 Henry M. Leland reorganized the failing Henry Ford Company and renamed it after the founder of Detroit, Antoine de la Mothe Cadillac. Leland had earned his reputation in precision machining and he brought these skills to his new car company, making Cadillac the "Standard of the World." In 1909 General Motors acquired the marque. As one of America's premier luxury builders with an unsurpassed V-16 engine, Cadillac's solid reputation carried it through the Great Depression of the early 1930s. In early 1942 Cadillac stopped passenger car production, and M-5 tanks and aircraft engines began rolling off its Detroit assembly lines. With more than 100,000 cars on back order by 1946, however, it would take two more years for postwar models to appear.

1947 CADILLAC 6207
CLUB COUPÉ

Like Buick, Cadillac introduced fresh prewar designs in 1942, which continued through 1947. These elegant cars featured striking pontoon fenders that stretched toward the front doors. The aerodynamic club coupé or "sedanette," was the most beautiful of the series, featuring a sloping roofline and boat tail tapered trunk.

[pages 36–37, 40]

1948 CADILLAC 6207
CLUB COUPÉ

Bill Mitchell, the designer who worked with Harley Earl, returned to the Cadillac Studio after World War II and refined the marque's prewar designs in 1947. The following year, he added tail fins—a design change that made the rear of the car as important as the front. Derived from the

Lockheed P-38 Lightning fighter, the tail fin became the definitive design treatment of the 1950s and in Mitchell's words, "established a longstanding Cadillac styling hallmark."

[pages 8, 38–39, 41]

1953 CADILLAC
ELDORADO CONVERTIBLE

The 1953 Eldorado was Cadillac's limited-edition prestige convertible. The windshield was a cut-down, "panoramic" design, and the convertible top stowed completely beneath a hard metal trunk. With a $7,750 price tag, the convertible was Detroit's most expensive production car. Only 532 cars were sold.

[page 100]

1957 CADILLAC
ELDORADO BROUGHAM

Like the Eldorado, the Brougham continued the trend of expensive, limited production cars. At more than $13,000, it was $3,000 pricier than Lincoln's Continental MkII, and as such, found only four hundred buyers. But the Brougham was Harley Earl's tour de force, featuring a pillarless, brushed aluminum roof, center opening doors, and for the first time, quadruple headlights. The model also had air suspension—a first for passenger cars—but it quickly proved difficult and costly to maintain. Within four years, the Brougham was restyled by Pininfarina in Italy. These cars, however, also experienced manufacturing problems and as a result, only two hundred were produced.

[pages 180–181]

1959 Cadillac Series 62
Convertible

1959 Cadillac Eldorado
Seville Hardtop

1959 Cadillac 60 Special
Fleetwood

1959 CADILLAC

Whether designed as a Series 62 Convertible, Eldorado Seville, or 60 Special Fleetwood, the 1959 Cadillacs will forever be remembered for their fins—the tallest, most dramatic automotive element of the 1950s. Presented as a "classic achievement in elegance and majesty of styling," Cadillac's chief designer, David Holls, added twin rocket-ship taillights to complete the look.

[pages 236, 237, 238, 239, 240–241, 242]

Facing a wave of financial losses, William C. Durant lost control of General Motors in 1910, just two years after he founded the company. In 1912 he partnered with famous Buick racecar driver Louis Chevrolet to create a line of upscale passenger cars that he hoped would give him the capital he needed to resume command of GM. The following year, Durant changed tacks and began building less expensive cars as a way of increasing volume. Chevrolet left in protest, but Durant succeeded in regaining control of GM when it bought the operating assets of Chevrolet, making it a division of the company in 1919. Within eight years, Chevrolet was the largest car manufacturer in the world. The marque ruled the low-priced market from 1931 to 1959, outselling its rival, Ford, for twenty-six of the twenty-eight years.

Like the other General Motors divisions, Chevrolet used prewar tooling through 1948, introducing its first postwar designs in 1949. These cars were conservative and sold well, but were nothing compared to the stylish and powerful mid-1950s models, which boasted a 265 cubic-inch V-8 engine, the now famous "small block."

1955 CHEVROLET NOMAD

General Motors showcased the Corvette Nomad at the Waldorf-Astoria hotel in New York City in 1954. Crowds loved the unusual two-door car, and as a result of the positive feedback, Harley Earl assigned Carl Renner to redesign the Chevrolet Bel Air station wagon. The result was the wonderful Chevrolet Nomad. It featured headlight "eyebrows," a waffle pattern interior, a ribbed roof, and distinctive "B" pillars. Nomads were Chevrolet's most expensive cars at $2,571.

[pages 133, 134–135]

1956 Chevrolet Two-Ten Sport Coupé

1956 Chevrolet Bel Air Convertible

1956 CHEVROLET

The 1956 Chevrolets continued the styling of the 1955 models. The Two-Ten was Chevrolet's mid-line model, priced between the low-end One-Fifty and the pricier Bel Air. More than 737,000 Two-Ten cars were built—but only 18,000 of those were sport coupés. The Bel Air was Chevrolet's premier offering, with many power and convenience options available. More than 668,000 Bel Airs were built, bringing total Chevrolet production to over 1.5 million units—and giving Chevrolet control of 27 percent of the American automobile market.

[pages 136, 137, 138, 139, 140–141, 142–143]

1957 CHEVROLET BEL AIR CONVERTIBLE

The 1957 model featured a fuel injected, 283 cubic inch V-8 engine that produced 283 horsepower—one horsepower per cubic inch of displacement. The basic body was carried over from 1955, but brighter details and colors freshened the car's appearance. This updated model was built in even greater numbers than the 1955 car, with more than 700,000 units sold.

[pages 176, 177]

1958 CHEVROLET BEL AIR IMPALA COUPÉ

In 1958, GM completely redesigned the Bel Air, adding two and a half inches to the wheelbase, new quadruple headlights, and graceful wings along the trunk. The car also made great use of aluminum trim, while its triple taillights indicated the high-end Impala model.

[pages 186–187, 188–189, 214]

1959 Chevrolet Impala Convertible

1959 Chevrolet Impala Sport Coupé

1959 CHEVROLET IMPALA

In October 1958, Chevrolet introduced its 1959 models. These cars, which were longer, lower, and wider, were a radical departure from the more conventionally proportioned cars of the previous year. Their most distinguishing feature, however, was the rear design of "cat's eye" taillights set under giant "brows." The Impala Convertible, Chevrolet wrote, boasted "authentic convertible glamour," while the sport coupé touted a "sparkling, crisp-lined hardtop highlighted by wrap-over back window for an almost unlimited rear view."

[pages 212–213, 215, 218, 220–221]

Harley Earl wanted to build a sports car to rival the British Jaguar XK120. To that end, he created the Corvette to be shown at the GM Motorama show car circuit in 1953. The little two-seater was received with such enthusiasm that it was immediately rushed into production. As Chevrolet's performance leader for more than fifty years, the Corvette has led the way as "America's Sports Car."

1953 CHEVROLET CORVETTE

On June 10, 1953, the first of 315 cars left the Flint, Michigan, assembly line. Relying heavily upon the Chevrolet parts bin, the Corvette featured a stock frame that was shortened thirteen inches and equipped with a 235 cubic inch, 6-cylinder engine mated to a two-speed Powerglide automatic transmission. Unfortunately, the car's unique, hand-built, fiberglass body was constructed without door handles or roll-up windows—providing a less than luxurious setting for Chevrolet's most expensive car.

[pages 85, 87]

1957 CHEVROLET CORVETTE

Engineer Zora Arkus-Duntuv first put a V-8 in Corvette's restyled 1956 model. But it wasn't until 1957 that the Corvette finally got the power to match its aggressive looks. This model's fuel-injected 283 cubic inch V-8 engine put out an impressive 283 horsepower, enabling drivers to accelerate from zero to sixty miles per hour in just 5.7 seconds.

[pages 222–223]

1960 CHEVROLET CORVETTE

The 1960 Corvette lost its previous "big tooth" grille and rounded rear fenders, but gained quadruple headlights and more powerful engines that exceeded 300 horsepower. That year, more than ten thousand units were sold, ensuring a solid future for Corvette.

[pages 227, 230–231]

CHRYSLER
The United States

CISITALIA
Italy

CUNNINGHAM
The United States

Walter Percy Chrysler founded Chrysler Corporation in 1924 after spending twenty years working for other manufacturers. In 1928 he purchased the Dodge Brothers Company and launched Plymouth and De Soto, making Chrysler one of the "Big Three" U.S. automakers. Then in 1934 Chrysler took a chance on the aerodynamic Airflow, whose advanced styling presented slanted radiators and windshields, enclosed headlights, and all-steel framework. Although the Airflow proved too radical and production ended just three years later, the impact on postwar Chrysler designs was tremendous.

1948 CHRYSLER TOWN & COUNTRY CONVERTIBLE

Chrysler continued with prewar designs until 1949, its product mainstay the Town & Country. The 1947 model—available in coupé and convertible styles—was based on the 1941 Town & Country station wagon, which had ash framing and mahogany panels. These were the first wagons that boasted passen-ger car styling rather than the boxy, truck-like designs from other manufacturers. Like their prewar predecessors, however, they still used structural wood framing, shaped plywood panels, and Hylander wool interiors. [page 32]

1955 Chrysler Imperial "Keller" Convertible

1955 Chrysler Imperial

1955 CHRYSLER IMPERIAL

For more than two decades, the Imperial was Chrysler's top-of-the-line car. In 1955, it became a separate division to rival Cadillac and Lincoln. To give these cars fresh appeal, styling chief Virgil Exner designed an elegant new shape called the "Forward Look." All the 1955 cars were hardtops except for the special convertible built for Kaufman T. Keller, Chrysler's chairman. Keller used his own styling skills to alter Exner's design, using a shortened wheelbase, a lower, wraparound windshield, and a continental kit for the spare tire. Many of Keller's changes were reflected in later Imperials.
[pages 144–145, 146, 147, 148, 149, 151, 152, 153]

1957 Chrysler 300C

1958 Chrysler 300D Convertible

CHRYSLER 300

Defined by its "hemi" engine, the Chrysler 300 literally meant 300 horsepower. The original 1955 car was built on a New Yorker hardtop chassis and featured a number of details from the upscale Imperial. In 1956, the model continued as the 300B, and with the debut of the 300C and 300D in subsequent years, the "letter car" was born. The 1957 model contained a new Virgil Exner body with Chrysler's biggest fins to date, replacing the quieter designs of the previous year. The car also featured power increases—maintaining its reputation as the fastest and most powerful production line vehicle in America.
[pages 4, 170–171, 172–173]

Piero Dusio, a former soccer star and amateur sports car racer, founded Consorzio Industriale Sportiva Italia in 1939 to produce sports equipment. After a string of profitable years, Dusio turned his attention in 1946 to building a light, quick single-seat racecar with Fiat power. Two-seat racing coupés and open cars soon followed, and by 1947, the marque debuted a Pininfarina-designed road car in both coupé and cabriolet models. While small, these cars were beautiful: The 202 Gran Sport is in New York's Museum of Modern Art.

1947 CISITALIA 202SM "NUVOLARI SPYDER"

The Cisitalia's spectacular, aerodynamic body featured Fiat 1100 running gear, which unfortunately made for ordinary performance in an otherwise advanced, hand-built car. Styled in smooth, flowing lines, the car's highlights included sweeping rear "fins," which were later seen in other limited production cars of the 1950s.
[pages 20, 21]

Briggs Swift Cunningham was a wealthy American sportsman and racecar driver. He was also the country's first postwar sports car manufacturer. Cunningham's lifetime goal was to win the prestigious LeMans twenty-four-hour race—but he preferred to do it in a car of his own. In 1951 he began building his dream car. The C-1 was his first prototype, followed by the racing C-2Rs. The next model, the C-3, was a passenger car—Cunningham's attempt to gain manufacturer status at LeMans. But the car was heavy—3,500 pounds—and expensive at $10,000. After five short years, production ended and Cunningham never realized his dream.

CUNNINGHAM
Continued

DE SOTO
The United States

DODGE
The United States

1952 CUNNINGHAM C-4RK

The C-4RK coupé and two C-4 roadsters raced at the 1952 LeMans. The cars were lighter and more powerful than their predecessors had been in 1951, and the coupé led for the first lap. Its finish was less than spectacular, but another Cunningham roadster, co-driven by Briggs Cunningham and Bill Spear, finished fourth overall and best in its class. The "K" designation on the coupé stands for Dr. Wuniblad Kamm, who discovered that a chopped tail improved aerodynamics.
[page 78]

Walter P. Chrysler created De Soto and Plymouth in 1928 to expand his young company's product line. The De Soto was priced just below the top-of-the-line Chrysler, while the Plymouth was marketed at the bottom of the range. Chrysler's plan worked well. De Soto proved to be an attractive—and popular—performance car until production stopped on February 9, 1942. After World War II, Chrysler scaled back on the number of models in its lineup but still offered the De Soto in interesting Suburban, taxi-cab, and Carry-All styles. In the 1950s, however, De Soto faced stiff competition with Dodge and Imperial crowding the top tier. When Chrysler moved down-market, the De Soto—designed as a slightly cheaper alternative to the once-highbrow Chrysler—began to flounder. The marque ended production in 1961.

1956 DE SOTO ADVENTURER

In 1955, the De Soto was revamped as a part of Chrysler's new "Forward Look" design. As a result, most 1956 De Sotos had minimal upgrades. The marque's one new stand-out, however, was its limited-edition Adventurer. Available only as a two-door hardtop, the Adventurer had a 320 horsepower engine and gold-anodized wheel covers. With numerous gold accents inside and out, the Adventurer was De Soto's most expensive and exclusive car.
[pages 150, 154, 155]

1959 DE SOTO ADVENTURER CONVERTIBLE

All Chrysler cars were designed with pronounced fins in 1957, a body style that continued through 1959. The car's unusual swivel seats were covered in white and gold Nylon Casino Corde and "handsome vinyl." De Soto's Adventurer was, according to Chrysler, "pure gold—in ride, pride, and pleasure."
[page 175]

During the turn of the twentieth century, machinists John and Horace Dodge supplied bicycle and automobile components to manufacturers from their small shop. After supplying Oldsmobile and Ford with engines and gear-boxes, they produced their first car under the name "Dodge Brothers" in 1914. Fourteen years later, Walter P. Chrysler bought the company for $170 million in order to offer a less expensive alternative to his regular product line. After the war, Dodge continued its reputation for producing solid, yet unspectacular transportation. In fact, it wasn't until 1953—when Virgil Exner began styling the cars and new performance engines appeared—that the marque became competitive on the racetrack.

1954 DODGE FIREARROW

The concept cars of the 1950s paved the way for the 1954 Firearrow, Exner's vehicle for introducing excitement to the marque. Of the four Firearrows produced, three were open cars and one was a closed coupé built on 1954 Dodge production running gear. All were built by Ghia, who had produced previous show cars for Chrysler.
[page 103]

DUAL MOTORS
The United States

FERRARI
Italy

FIAT
Italy

Dual Motors existed for a brief eight years, but in that time, the marque was able to combine the essence of Virgil Exner's American design and Ghia's Italian coachwork. The firm was founded when Eugene Casaroll bought the Chrysler Firebomb prototype and decided to go into production with a similar design. His cars were based on a modified Dodge chassis and a 315 cubic inch V-8 engine. But the cost to build exceeded the selling price, and less than two hundred cars were produced.

1956 DUAL GHIA
CONVERTIBLE COUPÉ

Frank Sinatra and other Hollywood stars were among those attracted to this beautiful, open four-seater. Here, designer Paul Farago altered the basic Exner design and created a more practical, comfortable car. With Connolly leather interior and a handmade Ghia body, this elegant car was quite different from the large, overly detailed offerings from American manufacturers.
[pages 79, 113]

Enzo Ferrari saw his first race in 1908 at age ten. By 1920 he had joined Alfa Romeo as a mechanic and racecar driver. He formed the legendary Scuderia Ferrari team in 1929 and successfully campaigned Alfa Romeo's racecars, which he signified by a black horse that pranced in a yellow shield. In 1940 Ferrari produced his first cars under the name Auto Avio Costruzioni—the name "Ferrari" was still under contract to Alfa Romeo. But his Maranello factory was severely damaged during the war and was not rebuilt until 1947. At that time, Gioachino Colombo was brought in to design the first car under the Ferrari name. The firm went on to build some of the greatest racecars and road cars in the world.

1949 FERRARI 166MM
"BARCHETTA"

The 166MM was Ferrari's first production car. It was introduced at the 1948 Turin Motor show, where the public nicknamed the car "Barchetta" or "Little Boat." The body was designed by Carlo Felice "Cici" Anderloni and built at his Carrozzeria Touring facility. Other coachbuilders from Bertone to Vignale produced handsome bodies for the 166MM, the first of many great Ferraris.
[pages 52, 53, 54]

1953 FERRARI 375MM

Constructed by Pininfarina as an open two-seater, the 375MM is one in a succession of beautiful V-12 Ferrari sports racing cars that were built in the 1950s. The potent 4.5-litre V-12 engine produced well over 300 horsepower. A "Competition Coupé" was also built in an unsuccessful attempt to win the LeMans twenty-four-hour race.
[pages 80, 81]

1958 FERRARI 250 TESTA
ROSSA

The famed Testa Rossa, or "Red Head," derives its name from the red crackle-finish on camshaft covers of its 3-litre V-12 engine. The car's unusual front section, its most distinguishing feature, was redesigned in later years for improved stability at high speeds. Less than thirty of these pontoon-fendered, Scaglietti-bodied racecars were built.
[pages 190, 191, 192–193, 206]

Fabbrica Italiana di Automobili Torino, or "Fiat," was created on July 11, 1899, by a group of investors intrigued with the possibilities of the automobile. Their leader, Giovanni Agnelli, enriched the marque by diversifying into other modes of transportation: airplanes, locomotives, and ships. Agnelli also gave the Italian firm a worldwide presence by acquiring manufacturing facilities throughout Europe and Asia. In 1936 Fiat produced its first mass-produced small car, the Fiat 500 or "Topolino." Agnelli's association with antifascists as the war progressed spared the company and allowed limited production to continue through the war years. Small cars proved to be Fiat's strong suit, and millions of postwar vehicles were produced.

1959 FIAT ABARTH
RECORD MONZA BIALBERO
ZAGATO

Karl Abarth was a European motorcycle champion in the 1930s. Years later, he began designing automobiles, making them like his beloved motorcycles: light, fast, and nimble. Abarths were built using modified Fiat running gear; the most famous ones featured Zagato bodies with "twin bubble" roofs.

[pages 198, 211]

From pocket watches to farm equipment, Henry Ford was inquisitive about all things mechanical. He experimented with his first car, the Quadricycle, in 1896, and formed the Ford Motor Company in 1903. Within two years, Ford had three hundred employees making twenty-five cars each day. Built on the conservative Model T and Model A, Ford's popularity exploded. By 1916 the marque was producing 734,811 cars per year—five times more than its biggest competitor. Henry Ford was a well-known pacifist, but when Pearl Harbor was attacked, he quickly turned the company's resources to military production. As the war wound down, Ford resumed its battle with Chevrolet for supremacy in the American automobile market. Its first postwar cars rolled off the assembly line on July 3, 1945.

1947 FORD WOODY
WAGON DELUXE

The pent-up demand for cars gave Ford 300,000 orders within the first two days of production in 1946. As expected, the cars were carry-over models from 1942. Real change did not appear until 1949.

[pages 28–29]

1955 Ford Thunderbird

1956 Ford Thunderbird

FORD THUNDERBIRD

Ford decided to build a small, "personal" car to rival Chevrolet's Corvette. The Frank Hershey–designed Thunderbird was an elegant solution; clean and simple, the two-seater came with a removable hardtop. The car was introduced in 1955 and sold 16,155 units the first year—a great success for Ford. The T-Bird was truly a car in which to be seen: The 1956 version featured a rear-mounted continental kit and a distinctive porthole in the hardtop.

[pages 114–115, 162, 163]

1956 FORD CROWN
VICTORIA SKYLINER

Ford redesigned its product line for 1955, making the cars longer, lower, and wider. This basic look carried over to 1956. The "B" pillar featured an over-the-roof sash, with the front portion of the roof made of glass. Just 603 Skyliners were sold, ending the run of glass-top cars for Ford.

[pages 158, 159, 160, 161]

1957 FORD FAIRLANE
500 SKYLINER

Ford's 1957 product line was redesigned with more aggressive styling and trim. This model was available as a convertible or "retractable" hardtop that stowed completely in the massive trunk.

[page 174]

FRAZER NASH
England

GENERAL MOTORS
The United States

HUDSON
The United States

Frazer Nash was a small automotive builder founded by British Captain Archibald Frazer-Nash in 1924. Early versions were unusual, chain-driven open two-seaters that appeared regularly at sports car competitions. Right before World War II, the firm—now controlled by the Aldington brothers—began importing BMWs from Germany. This relationship eventually led the company to produce postwar models powered by BMW 2-litre engines. Over the next thirty-three years, only four hundred cars were made.

1954 FRAZER NASH
LEMANS COUPÉ

In 1949 Norman Culpan and H. J. Aldington drove the Frazer Nash roadster to a third-place finish at LeMans. The LeMans replica became the firm's best-known model. Eight cars were built with a handsome aluminum coupé body. Production ended in 1957 with a scant eighty-four cars produced after the war.
[pages 82, 91]

William Crapo Durant began his career in 1886 building lightweight carts. By 1904 his manufacturing experience and business acumen led him to become the general manager at Buick Motor Company. Durant quickly turned Buick into the nation's top-selling marque. Durant went on to create the world's largest industrial company, General Motors, by adding Cadillac, Oldsmobile, Oakland (later renamed Pontiac), and eventually, Chevrolet. In 1920 Alfred P. Sloan Jr. took command of the company and eventually coordinated the independent divisions into a more efficient and cohesive corporation. He also enticed renowned designer Harley Earl to become GM's first styling chief in 1927, thus creating the company's famed Art & Colour Section.

Earl's designs had tremendous impact on the automotive industry. In 1938 his team created the first "dream car," the Buick Y-Job. The car was presented to the financial community at the Waldorf-Astoria hotel in New York City. After World War II, these lavish exhibitions became open to the public and were dubbed "Motorama." They continued until 1961.

1959 FIREBIRD III

Motorama cars excited the public and offered a glimpse into the future. The 1959 theme of the exhibition, "Imagination in Motion," was showcased in the Firebird III. This jet-airplane styled car was loaded with space-age advances such as special drag brakes that emerged from flat panels to slow the car when it was moving at high speeds, an automated guidance system to avoid accidents, and "no hold" steering. Other, more realistic features—cruise control, ultrasonic keys, instrument warning lights, and temperature control—would not become standard until forty years later.
[pages 234–235]

Hudson was formed in 1909 by a group of former Oldsmobile engineers in Detroit. Led by Roy D. Chapin, the company was named after its chief benefactor, Joseph L. Hudson. The Hudson Motor Car Company was just one of many American manufacturers in the mid-priced field. Like the other marques, Hudson ceased automobile production during the war, debuting its new designs in 1948, a year earlier than most manufacturers. These sleek cars featured a new "step-down" chassis, which gave the car a lower center of gravity, improving handling and increasing interior space. In spite of the success of this design, Hudson could not hold on to its market share and merged with Nash in 1953 to form American Motors Corporation. Four years later, AMC dropped Hudson from its model line.

1951 HUDSON HORNET

The Hornet was introduced in 1951 and featured Hudson's special high-compression engine with an aluminum "Power Dome" cylinder head. The car's "severe usage" options further enhanced its performance and led to a successful stock car racing season, with wins in twelve out of forty-one NASCAR Grand National races. Drivers included Marshall Teague, Tim Flock, and Herb Thomas.
[pages 70–71, 72–73, 75]

JAGUAR
England

LANCIA
Italy

William Lyons and William Walmsley founded the Swallow Sidecar Company in 1928. Soon they were producing sporting bodies for the popular European car marques. Their first car, the SS-90, was introduced in 1935. The Jaguar Saloon appeared the following year. The company changed its name to Jaguar in March 1945, eschewing the unpleasant World War II "S.S." association. The first postwar designs— the Mark V Saloon and Drop Head Coupé— appeared in 1948, but it was the high-performance sports cars of the 1950s that would give the marque legendary status.

1952 Jaguar XK120 Open Two-Seater Convertible

1952 Jaguar XK120 Fixed Head Coupé

JAGUAR XK120

The XK120 was first shown at London's Earls Court Motor Show in October 1948. It was a picture of elegance, with an ash frame and aluminum body. The number "120" was a reference to the car's top speed—a figure easily achieved by its powerful 3.5-litre, 6-cylinder engine. Lyons did not anticipate the tremendous response to his beautiful, open two-seater; he had intended to build just two hundred units. But public demand led to a six-year production run of more than twelve thousand cars. Over the next several years, the company added an equally stunning fixed head coupé and a luxurious drop head coupé to the series.

[pages 55, 56–57, 58–59]

1956 JAGUAR 3.4 SALOON

In the late 1930s, Jaguar solidified its reputation, building beautiful, flowing saloon-bodied cars. After the war, the marque split its attention between continuing the prewar saloons and constructing new sports cars. In 1956 Jaguar introduced a new saloon with unitary construction. Designed by Lyons, the car retained Jaguar's well-known curvaceous lines and athletic performance.

[pages 122–123]

Vincenzo Lancia was a young mechanic and race-car driver for Fiat when he chose to start his own company in 1906. From the start, Lancias were known for their innovation and performance. In 1922 Lancia patented unitary construction based on his observations of the structural benefits of a ship's hull design—creating from those plans the noteworthy Lancia Lambda. The Aprilia, which debuted in the late 1930s, was a dynamic, futuristic car that boasted the benefits of fully independent suspension and wind tunnel testing. The marque's factory in Turin, Italy, had been bombed during the war, but the company was able to restart production on the Aprilia in 1945. The equally beautiful 1950s Aurelia models continued the Lancia tradition.

1957 LANCIA AURELIA

Aurelia, successor to the Aprilia, was announced to the public in 1950 and continued production until 1958. It was first offered in saloon, limousine, and coupé styles. The Aurelia convertible with body by Pininfarina was launched in 1955. More than sixteen thousand units were built during the model's eight-year run.

[pages 196, 199]

LINCOLN
The United States

MERCEDES-BENZ
Germany

In 1917 Henry M. Leland left Cadillac over a dispute with William C. Durant, the head of General Motors. Leland went on to create Lincoln, which produced its first car in 1920. By 1922, however, the new marque was struggling financially and was bought by Henry Ford at the request of his son Edsel. After Ford acquired Lincoln, the marque produced some of the greatest cars of the classic era—most notably the V-12 Zephyr and the Continental, both designed by E. T. "Bob" Gregorie. Lincoln's first postwar cars were identical to the 1942 models. It wasn't until 1949 that restyled models with V-8 engines were introduced.

1956 CONTINENTAL MK II

After a seven-year absence, Lincoln revived the Continental name to do battle with Cadillac and Imperial. Initially, Continental was launched as a separate division of Ford Motor Company, but after four years it became part of the Lincoln group. The Ford Special Products team, which included John Reinhart, Gordon Buehrig, and Bob Thomas, designed this elegant two-door coupé. But because the Mk II was mostly hand-built, Ford lost $1,000 per car, despite its steep $10,000 sticker price. [PAGES 164, 165, 166, 167]

1956 LINCOLN PREMIERE

Unlike most manufacturers, Lincoln delayed redesigning its models in 1955, instead revealing a whole new look for its 1956 fleet. These cars were seven inches longer, three inches wider, and had sharp, angular lines. Lincoln sold fifty thousand cars—a solid number for the first year, but still only a third of its rival Cadillac's sales. [pages 10, 156, 157]

The Daimler and Benz companies had been building cars independently since 1885, but Germany's economic hardship after World War I brought the two firms together in 1926. In the late 1920s and 1930s, the newly merged company worked with talented automotive engineer Ferdinand Porsche to create the legendary S, SS, and SSK models. Like many German manufacturers, the firm had strong ties to the Nazi regime, initially becoming associated with the party through Grand Prix racing and the production of vehicles for military use. Its major facilities sustained heavy damage during the war, but the marque was able to quickly resume production for its utilitarian 170V model in early 1946. The first postwar vehicles were built for commercial use, with passenger car production commencing the following year. By 1949 vehicle output had surpassed prewar levels.

1953 MERCEDES-BENZ 300S CABRIOLET

Mercedes-Benz reentered the luxury market in 1951 with the beautifully crafted 300 series, which retained the elegance of the prewar 500K and 540K models. At the 1951 Frankfurt show, the marque unveiled its 300S version—the most expensive German cars of the time. The S cars used a shortened wheelbase and an upgraded twin carburetor engine. First offered as both a coupé and cabriolet, the 300S was built in various body styles until 1962. [page 97]

1955 Mercedes-Benz 300SL Alloy Coupé

1956 Mercedes-Benz 300SL Coupé

1958 Mercedes-Benz 300SL Roadster

MERCEDES BENZ 300SL

One of the greatest designs in automotive history was the 1954 Mercedes-Benz 300SL Coupé. Affectionately referred to as the "Gullwing," the 300SL was built as the road version of the marque's 1952 LeMans-winning racecar. The car's most unusual styling feature—the unique roof-hinged doors—was more than

MERCEDES-BENZ
Continued

MERCURY
The United States

MG
England

NASH
The United States

cosmetic; they were integral to the structural design of the car as well. Approximately 1,400 coupés were produced in steel, with twenty-nine bodies built in aluminum alloy for racing. In 1957, in response to public demand, Mercedes-Benz created the 300SL Roadster. This car replaced the coupé, but only 1,900 Roadsters were completed by the end of production in 1964. [pages 116–117, 118, 119, 120, 121]

Edsel Ford created Mercury in 1939 to fill the gap between the high-end Lincolns and the high-volume Fords. Originally built on the Ford chassis, Mercury became part of the newly formed Lincoln Mercury Division after the war. When production resumed in late 1945, raw materials were still in short supply and some cars were delivered incomplete—often, railroad planks replaced bumpers. Mercury increased its range of cars as the 1950s continued.

1948 MERCURY
CONVERTIBLE

The 1948 Mercury was almost identical to the 1946 and 1947 models, which in turn were facelifted 1942 designs. More than fifty thousand coupés, sedans, convertibles, and wood-sided station wagons were built, making Mercury the tenth best-selling American car. [pages 30–31]

In the early 1920s, Morris Garages in Oxford, England, began producing its own roadster. Over the next twenty years, these wonderful little cars enjoyed success both on the road and the track. In September 1933 Tazio Nuvolari won the Ulster Tourist Trophy in an MG K3 Magnette, setting a lap record that would stand for eighteen years. The firm shifted production from cars to Albemarle bomber parts in September 1939, but MG was back in the automobile business— using prewar designs— by 1945. The new MG-TC was an instant hit with American servicemen stationed in England. During its four-year model run, ten thousand "TCs" were built.

1958 MGA Roadster

1958 MGA Coupé

1958 MGA

The MGA was introduced in 1955 as a replacement for the nineteen-year-old T-series. MG finally had a car with the looks, handling, and performance of a modern automobile. More than 101,000 cars were built in coupé and roadster form, with production ending in 1962. [pages 202, 203]

In 1917 Charles W. Nash formed his own motorcar company after leaving as president of General Motors. A smart businessman, Nash steered his company through the turmoil of the Great Depression, eventually merging with appliance manufacturer Kelvinator. In 1941 Nash unveiled the economical 600, named for its ability to travel six hundred miles on a twenty-gallon gas tank. Nash quickly resumed production after the war, updating its 1942 models in 1945. As the 1940s progressed, the Big Three manufacturers regained their production capability, and Nash moved into its own niche of building unconventional, economical transportation.

**1947 NASH AMBASSADOR
SUBURBAN**

Like the 1942 models, the 1946 to 1948 Nashes featured a wide horizontal grille. The Suburban, however, contained wooden panels that were added to its fastback sedan body. The car was attractive but expensive. During its three-year run, only 1,000 units were produced. Nash did not produce updated designs on the Suburban until 1949.

[pages 22–23, 24, 25, 26, 27]

1953 NASH HEALEY

In 1951 Donald Healey assisted Nash in creating a small sporting car. The Nash Healey used a Nash overhead valve 6-cylinder engine with Panelcraft

bodies built in England. The following year, the chassis was wrapped in a sporting body by Pininfarina. Yet the car never gained a following and production ended in 1954.

[pages 84, 86, 88]

**1956 NASH
METROPOLITAN**

The Metropolitan was another quirky car brought to market by Nash in 1953. The car looked like a miniature Nash and was intended to compete with the new, smaller European models. Chrome molding was added in 1956, and the "two-tone" Metropolitan was born. Despite being plagued by rust and poor handling, more than 100,000 units were sold over its eight-year production run.

[pages 128–129]

Oldsmobile was founded by Ransom Eli Olds in 1896 and was the longest-running American marque, ending production in May 2004. Olds left in 1904 to form REO, but the firm continued on, becoming part of General Motors in November 1908. From the start, Oldsmobile was successful. In its early years, it was the world's largest car manufacturer. It carved out a reputation through the 1920s and 1930s with technical refinements such as four-wheel brakes, chromium plating, synchromesh transmissions, and downdraft carburetion. The marque began producing new cars again in July 1945, albeit modified 1942 models. It wasn't until 1949 that it brought out new designs, which featured high-compression Rocket V-8 engines. This enabled Oldsmobile to become a leader on the racetrack, winning numerous NASCAR events and the first La Carrera Panamericana.

**1957 OLDSMOBILE SUPER
88 CONVERTIBLE**

Oldsmobiles were given new bodies in 1957. These models, like their predecessors, had rocket-like details above the headlights and jet engine taillights. The hot J-2 engine option also offered plenty of "rocket" power. This 312 horsepower V-8 was immediately successful in the stock cars driven by Lee Petty and Richard Petty. This powerful engine was soon banned from NASCAR, though, forcing Oldsmobile to withdraw from stock car racing.

[pages 178–179, 185]

Brothers Ernesto, Ettore, and Bindo Maserati sold the Maserati company to the Orsi family in 1938, but for a decade, they remained with the firm as engineering consultants. In order to get back to what they loved most— building light, fast sports cars—they formed Officina Specializzata Costruzione Automobili in 1947. These cars featured small-displacement engines that were so effective that one early model won the 1100cc class at the 1950 Mille Miglia. The marque's greatest victory occurred when Sterling Moss placed first overall at the 1954 Sebring twelve-hour race. But the little company survived just twenty years and sold its assets to M. V. Augusta in 1967.

1957 O.S.C.A. S187

O.S.C.A. was a small family company that intentionally produced no more than thirty cars per year. The S187 first appeared in 1956 and was fitted with a 749cc double overhead cam engine capable of 70 horsepower at 7,000 rpm. Built over a period of just three years, the sportsracer was designed with a number of distinctive, aerodynamic bodies, including those by Vignale, Zagato, and Morelli.

[pages 204–205, 207]

Since its founding by brothers James and William Packard in 1899, the marque had earned a solid reputation for building fine cars. Aimed at the well heeled, the Packard varied its styling only slightly prior to World War II—a strategy that at the time was considered appropriate for wealthier clientele. After the war, however, automobile marketing changed, and the public began to expect new designs more frequently. Packard, still a relatively small independent builder, could not keep up with this trend, and in 1954 was acquired by Studebaker. There, the marque languished. Its cars merely became repackaged Studebakers, and in 1958 Packard ceased production.

1950 PACKARD CUSTOM
EIGHT CONVERTIBLE

The 1949-1/2 through 1950 cars were called the "Golden Anniversary Packards." Even so, there were few visual clues to differentiate these cars from previous postwar models. The company introduced the Ultramatic automatic transmission in this 23rd Series, creating a lot of enthusiasm. These cars—with the so-called "pregnant elephant" look—would be replaced in 1951 with less expensive, more modern vehicles. Yet sales of these more economical Packards were still unable to keep the venerable company independent.

[pages 66, 68]

Walter P. Chrysler created Plymouth in 1928 to serve as a low-cost alternative to other Dodge and Chrysler products. Instantly the marque found its niche, battling Chevrolet and Ford in serviceable low-cost transportation. But Chrysler's divisions returned slowly to production after the war; the 1946 Plymouths had only minimal changes from the 1942 models. Postwar Plymouths were not particularly stylish or quick, and with limited revisions, the firm slipped in national sales rankings from third to fifth, behind Chevrolet, Ford, Buick, and Oldsmobile. In 1955, however, the new V-8 engines and "Forward Look" styling reenergized all Chrysler Corporation's products, including Plymouth. The crisp, sweeping lines of the new design returned Plymouth back to third place in sales, where it would remain Chrysler's volume leader for decades.

1954 PLYMOUTH
BELMONT

Virgil Exner's 1954 Belmont was a harbinger of the great changes that would come to Plymouth in 1955. This bright red roadster was designed to draw attention away from Chevrolet's Corvette. Both cars had curvaceous fiberglass bodies, seating for two, and wraparound windshields. But the Belmont was much larger, with a chrome V-8 engine and a luxurious, cocoonlike, leather interior. The Belmont joined the K-310, Adventurer, and Firearrow to become one of Exner's greatest designs.

[pages 6, 110–111, 112]

PONTIAC
The United States

PORSCHE
Germany

Alfred P. Sloan, president of General Motors, saw a gap in GM's product line between the inexpensive Chevrolet and the mid-priced Oldsmobile. In 1926 he created Pontiac to fill that void, and within three years it was the fifth best-selling marque in the United States. After World War II, Pontiac continued with its 1942 designs until its first major update in 1949. In 1955 the marque became more perform-ance-oriented. It received a Strato-Flight Hydra-Matic Drive automatic transmission, and was the last of the GM divisions to receive V-8 power—the 287-cubic-inch Strato Streak engine.

1957 PONTIAC STAR
CHIEF CUSTOM SAFARI
STATION WAGON

Semon E. "Bunky" Knudsen was appointed general manager of the Pontiac division in 1956. Knudsen continued to give Pontiac a younger, more athletic image. According to the compa-

ny's ads, one of its more popular models, the "Star Flight" styled Safari wag-ons, contained the "smooth flowing power of America's Number One Road Car plus the con-venience of space for up to nine passengers."

[pages 182, 183, 184]

1960 PONTIAC
BONNEVILLE CONVERTIBLE

The Bonneville was Pontiac's new high-performance model. Launched in 1957, it received the aggressive "Wide-Track" look two years later. In 1960 the model was upgraded with a Tempest 425 V-8 engine, which had a 4-barrel carburetor and put out an impressive 303 horsepower and 425 lb. ft. of torque. Leather inte-rior, a polished walnut dash, a clock, courtesy lamps, and "dual ash-trays" completed the list of luxury appointments.

[pages 216, 217]

The name Porsche is syn-onymous with high per-formance automobiles. But the family's role in auto-motive history predates even Porsche's beginning in 1948. Dr. Ferry Porsche, the founder of the marque, had worked with his father on the Volkswagen project in the late 1930s. Then after World War II he began developing a small sports car based on the rear-engine, air-cooled VW design. Fifty cars were built in his small shop in Gmund, Austria, before he moved to facilities outside Stuttgart. The firm's first car, the Porsche 356, was an immediate hit. A succession of powerful road and race cars were to follow.

1955 PORSCHE 550
SPYDER

In 1951 Porsche logged its first entry in the LeMans twenty-four hour race, winning its class with a modified produc-tion 356. The victory inspired Porsche to create a purpose-built racer—the 550 Spyder—in 1953.

Erwin Komenda designed the lightweight aluminum body and mounted a Type 547 4-cam, 4-cylinder engine in front of the rear axle. The Spyder was a very successful racecar, but it may best be known as the car actor James Dean died in while driving on a rural California highway.

[page 106]

1956 PORSCHE 356A
CARRERA SPEEDSTER

The legendary Porsche Speedster started as a lower priced, decontented version of the popular 356 model. This lighter car was offered with a variety of powerplants, including the 100 horse-power 4-cam engine bred in the 550 Spyder. The name "Carrera" was a nod to Porsche's success in the 1954 La Carrera Panamericana road race.

[page 197]

1958 PORSCHE 718 RSK

The RSK evolved from the 550 Spyder and continued to use the older model's 1.5 liter 4-cam engine. The RSK, however, featured a new front suspension, which lowered the body, generating better aerody-namics. These cars were very competitive, taking podium finishes at Sebring and the Targa Florio, and dominating its class at LeMans in 1958.

[pages 194–195]

1960 PORSCHE 356
CARRERA GT

In 1957 Porsche made two versions of the Carrera—the fully equipped Deluxe, and the Spartan, high performance GT. By 1960 Porsche had dropped the Deluxe, and the GT became the mar-que's only 356 model with the high-performance engine. These GTs were popular on the racetrack, where the loud, high-revving engines could be driven at high speeds.

[pages 208, 209]

ROLLS-ROYCE
England

SAAB
Sweden

One of the most revered names in automobiles dates back to 1904, when Charles Stewart Rolls agreed to sell the new 15 horsepower cars produced by Henry Royce. Together, their dedication to perfection led to the creation of the 1907 Silver Ghost—a car that raised the standard to which other cars aspired to be built. The firm's superior reputation continued with coach-built Phantoms through the 1930s. In 1938 Rolls-Royce built a new factory in Crewe, Chesire, to produce airplane engines. After the war, Crewe became the marque's new home for automobile production and remained so for more than sixty years.

1950 ROLLS-ROYCE
SILVER WRAITH
by Hooper

Tall, stately, and elegant, the postwar Rolls-Royces carried the familiar design themes of the prewar models—despite the postwar trend that was moving away from large, chauffeur driven, coach-built cars. As before, the Silver Wraith was produced to the highest standards, with beautiful handwork and great attention to detail.
[pages 60–61]

1951 ROLLS-ROYCE
SILVER DAWN

The Silver Dawn was the first Rolls-Royce built with a standard body, designed and produced in quantity by the Pressed Steel company. The car was created for the export

market and featured a shorter wheelbase, more flexible engine, and automatic transmission. Now, the owner-driver was Rolls-Royce's clientele.
[page 96]

1957 ROLLS-ROYCE
SILVER CLOUD I
by H. J. Mulliner

The beautiful Silver Cloud was first produced in 1955 and was offered with either a standard or an "upscale" custom coach-built body. The car was identical to the Bentley S-Type except for the radiator and "Spirit of Ecstasy" mascot. Several years later, Rolls-Royce introduced a new V-8 engine to the Silver Cloud II. By the time the Silver Cloud III ended the series run in 1966, a record number 7,365 "Clouds" had been produced.
[page 219]

Saab, like BMW, traces its lineage back to aircraft production. The firm flew its first plane, the Ju 86 bomber, in August 1939. As the need for military aircraft subsided, Svenska Aeroplan Aktiebolag Ltd.—or "Saab"—decided to use its capabilities to produce automobiles. While experienced in aeronautical design, the company's engineers lacked experience in passenger car production. So they borrowed heavily from the familiar, prewar DKW, which powered the front wheels with its two-stroke engine. They hired renowned Swedish industrial designer Sixten Sason, who styled the body with a dramatic airfoil shape. The firm began production on the first Saab in 1950, and it arrived in showrooms as the model "92," a name taken from its internal project number.

1959 SAAB 750GT

With confidence from its success on the road rally circuit, Saab engineers built the high-performance GT model in 1958. It was based on the Saab 93, which began production in December 1955. The GT was upgraded with a 45 horsepower triple-Solex carburetor 3-cylinder engine and a 4-speed transmission. Only 605 cars were built during its three-year production run.
[page 210]

STUDEBAKER
The United States

TATRA
Czechoslovakia

Brothers Henry and Clem Studebaker began their careers building wagons in South Bend, Indiana, in 1852. After becoming the largest maker of wagons in the world, they turned their attention and resources to automobile production in the late 1890s. They were equally successful in the car business, and by 1928 the marque was moving into the luxury car field with the acquisition of Pierce-Arrow. After World War II, Studebaker was the first to emerge with fresh designs, most notably, the "Coming or Going" look from Virgil Exner of the Raymond Loewy Studios. But Studebaker was much smaller and had fewer resources than the Big Three automobile makers, and in 1954 the company was forced to acquire Packard to keep pace. Despite producing a number of interesting cars after the merge, Studebaker ended automobile production in March 1966.

1952 STUDEBAKER COMMANDER CONVERTIBLE

In 1952 Studebaker celebrated its 100th anniversary by giving a fresh face to the "bullet-nose" design of the previous two years. But this minor redesign wasn't enough to lure new customers. That year, Studebaker's production dropped to two-thirds of its 1951 numbers. Priced at $2,548, the Commander Convertible was the firm's most expensive and prestigious offering, but only 1,715 cars were built.
[pages 67, 69]

1953 STUDEBAKER COMMANDER STARLINER

The "Loewy coupés," designed by Robert Bourke and Holden Koto under the direction of Raymond Loewy, made their debut in 1953. The low, wide cars had minimal chrome and were a dramatic departure from the other cars of the day. The Starliner model was honored by the New York Museum of Modern Art as one of the ten greatest postwar production automobiles.
[pages 90, 98, 99]

This Czechoslovakian automaker has a history of innovative, unusual designs that provide a fascinating glimpse into the automotive future. The firm traces its roots to 1897, but it did not manufacture under the name "Tatra" until 1923. Under the direction of designer Hans Ledwinka, the cars featured enclosed aerodynamic bodies with air-cooled rear engines. These features formed the basis of the "people's car"—later designed by Ferdinand Porsche. Tatra sued over what it believed were stolen patents, finally winning the suit after World War II hostilities ceased. Tatra was the only marque to build cars during the war years, and continued production until 1999.

1947 TATRA T87

Hans Ledwinka's T87 first appeared in 1936. It was an improvement upon his 1934 design of the T77. Though the T87 was in continuous production for the next fourteen years, just 3,023 cars were built. The car featured a number of unusual elements, giving the Tatra its otherworldly look. Highlights included the round front, enclosed bodywork, large central headlight, steeply sloping three-piece windshield, large rear airscoops, and a dramatic fin that rose from the tapered tail.
[pages 18–19]

TRIUMPH	TUCKER	VOLKSWAGEN
England	*The United States*	*Germany*

Triumph, founded in 1885, began as a bicycle manufacturer—then motorcycle producer—adding small, well-made cars in 1923. Sporting roadsters were introduced in the 1930s. But Triumph faced vigorous competition coupled with an inflated product line, and in 1939, the firm was forced into receivership. In 1944 Standard's Sir John Black purchased the Triumph name. Standard worked to move the Triumph name up-market, debuting its famed TR series of sports cars in 1953.

1955 Triumph TR2

1960 Triumph TR3A

TRIUMPH TR

The TR series was intended to battle MG, which had successfully exported sports cars to the U.S. Introduced in 1953, the TR2 was the first production TR and was based on the TRX concept vehicle from the 1950 Paris Motor Show. The series was popular, and over time the car became more sophisticated and powerful, culminating in the TR8 models of the late 1970s.

[pages 92, 93, 94–95]

The Tucker Corporation had a brief but controversial existence. The firm was created in 1946 by Preston Tucker. Working with designers Alex Tremulis, George S. Lawson, and J. Gordon Lippincott & Associates of New York, Tucker aspired to bring the most advanced postwar car to market. Tucker's dream was to merge safety, speed, and comfort into a stylish package, the likes of which had not been seen before. Plans called for mating a helicopter powerplant— a massive 592-cubic- inch air-cooled, fuel injected aluminum rear- engine—with the new "Tuckermatic" transmission. Despite having 300,000 advance orders and 1,000 dealers, the marque experienced financial troubles that led to an investigation by the U.S. government. By the time Preston Tucker was exonerated of fraud charges in 1950, his company, his car, and his dreams were dead.

1948 TUCKER

Promising to be the most innovative car of its time, many of the Tucker's advanced features ended up facing real-world technological problems. By the time production began, several of these special features were replaced with average parts. The big air-cooled engine was substituted with a much smaller, water-cooled 355 cubic-inch unit. The highly touted "Tuckermatic" was never installed, and was replaced by an old Cord preselect transmission. The final car, as advanced as it was, fell short of Preston Tucker's promises and only fifty-one of these streamlined sedans were ever built.

[pages 42–43]

Dr. Ferdinand Porsche, who wanted to build a car for the masses, first conceived the Volkswagen, or "People's Car," in the early 1930s. His original designs used Zundapp or NSU air-cooled motorcycle engines mounted in the rear. In 1933 his designs caught the attention of Adolf Hitler, who saw the automobile as crucial to the success of National Socialism. (The nickname "Beetle" has even been attributed to Hitler.) Dozens of prototypes were built and tested over the next six years before the first production cars left the Wolfsburg facilities on August 15, 1940. During wartime, the factory mostly produced the Jeep-like Kubelwagen and the amphibious Schwimmwagen. Even though the factory received significant damage during bombing raids and was placed under British control in 1945, production resumed immediately, and 522 cars were produced that year.

1950 VOLKSWAGEN

The small and inexpensive Volkswagen proved popular in postwar Europe. It received continual upgrades to the engine, brakes, transmission, and comfort features during its more than fifty-year production run. Overall, more than twenty-two million cars have been built, making the Volkswagen the most popular marque in the world.

[pages 33, 34–35]

LIST OF OWNERS

My first car was a 1957 Oldsmobile Fiesta Station Wagon. It was big, powerful, comfortable, and blue as the sky. My work on *Automobiles of the Chrome Age: 1946–1960* has allowed me to return to my youth, when each trip behind the wheel felt like it was the first time—a colorful memory that I now share with my children. With that, I'd like to thank the dedicated owners who have generously allowed me to photograph their cars, keeping these rolling memories of youth alive for us all:

Frank R. Allocca
Bernard Berman
George Bickel
Ed and Carol Blumenthal
Bill Borden
Ted Boyd
Ralph Brown
Nicola Bulgari
Robert Carnivale
Hank and Jane Casden
Richard and Pat Chappell
Ele Chesney
Miles Collier
Joseph Dillon
Robert Donatucci
Doug Dressler
Woody Dries
Gene and Marlene Epstein
Gary Ford
D. Craig Fuller
General Motors Corporation
Russ Gowdy
Saul Greenberg
Jay Hammond
Richard Herwig
Van and John Horneff
Bill Jacobson
Thomas and James Kidd
Richard and Jean Laird
Ralph Lauren
Mark Leiberman

Chip Loree
Bud and Thelma Lyon
Steve Maconi
Sam and Emily Mann
Dave Markel
David Mayo
Don Meluzio
Kris Mera
Chip Miller
Robert Mirably
Jack Morris
Richard and Nancy Myers
Steve Piaccio
Joe Puleo
Howard Pyle
Paul and Lois Reedy
Michael Riebe
R. Craig Rosenfeld
Len Rusiewicz
Sandy Sadtler
Joseph Santaniello
Donald Schneider
Robert Stockman
Richard Tabas
Noel Thompson
Michael G. Tillson, III
Hampton C. Wayt
Warren Weiner
Henry Wessells
Langdon Wheeler

SUGGESTED READINGS

Automobile Quarterly (various editions).

Banham, Russ. *The Ford Century: Ford Motor Company and the Innovations That Shaped the World.*
San Diego, California, Tehabi Books, 2002.

Berghoff, Bruce. *The GM Motorama: Dream Cars of the Fifties.*
Osceola, Wisconsin, Motorbooks International, 1995.

Burness, Tad. *Monstrous American Car Spotter's Guide: 1920–1980.*
Osceola, Wisconsin, Motorbooks International, 1986.

Chappell, Pat. *The Hot One Chevrolet: 1955–1957*, 3rd Edition.
Contoocook, New Hampshire, Dragonwyck Publishing, Ltd., 1988.

Editors of Consumer Guide. *Cars of the 40s.*
Skokie, Illinois, Publications International, Ltd., 1979.

Editors of Consumer Guide. *Cars of the 50s.*
Skokie, Illinois, Publications International, Ltd., 1978.

Edsall, Larry. *Concept Cars from the 1930s to the Present.*
New York, New York, Barnes & Noble Publishers, 2003.

Flammang, James M. and the editors of Consumer Guide.
Cars of the Fabulous 50s: A Decade of High Style and Good Times.
Lincolnwood, Illinois, Publications International, Ltd., 2002.

Flammang, James M. *Standard Catalog of Imported Cars, 1946–1990.*
Iola, Wisconsin, Krause Publications, Inc., 1992.

Georgano, Nick (ed). *The Beaulieu Encyclopedia of the Automobile.*
London, England, The Stationery Office, 2000.

Gunnell, John (ed). *Standard Catalog of American Cars, 1946–1975*, 3rd Edition.
Iola, Wisconsin, Krause Publications, Inc., 1992.

Lillywhite, David (ed). *The Encyclopedia of Classic Cars.*
San Diego, California, Thunder Bay Press, 2003.

Ludvigsen, Karl. *Porsche: Excellence Was Expected.*
Cambridge, Massachusetts, Bentley Publishers, 2003.

Moloney, James H. and George H. Dammann. *Encyclopedia of American Cars, 1946–1959.*
Sarasota, Florida, Crestline Publishing, 1980.

Oleski, Frank. *World Sports Cars, Series Built from 1945–1980.*
Basel, Germany, Motor Classic Verlag, 1987.

ACKNOWLEDGEMENTS

Automobiles of the Chrome Age was photographed exclusively in the studio, which required a large crew of talented professionals. My sincere gratitude goes to John Burzichelli and Esteban Granados of the Hill Studio, and to studio assistants Bill Wynes, Dave March, John Wynn, Dan Mezick, Mary Dunham, Steven Crossot, Joe D'Angeles, Bronwyn Smith, Ken Burgess, Adam Hoffman, Peter Grims, and Eric Furman.

One of the more difficult tasks in a project of this scope is locating the best cars and coordinating schedules with the owners. For their efforts I especially need to thank Robert DePue Brown, Mike Tillson, Ed Tatios, Keith Flickinger, Paul Russell, Janet Oliver, Jed Rapoport, Jonathan Stein, Phil Neff, Pat Chappell, Gene Epstein, Marty Wadkins, Debbie Fass, and Lois Reedy.

Allen Dugan, Mark Bofinger, and John Fetter have unselfishly provided decades of printing and production expertise to ensure the highest quality reproduction of my photographs. The majority of the images in this book were created digitally, using a Phase One Digital Capture back on either a Mamiya RZ67 or Sinar 4x5 camera. Kevin Raber of Phase One and Lance Schad of Systems Solutions Incorporated offered invaluable technical assistance that allowed me to fully utilize the benefits of this new technology.

I'd also like to thank Tehabi Books for believing in this project—President and Publisher Chris Capen and Senior Vice President Sam Lewis—and Christopher Sweet at Harry N. Abrams. Senior Art Director Josie Delker and Production Artist Monika Stout have once again transformed a group of automobile photographs into a beautiful book. "LandSpeed" Louise Ann Noeth has been a valuable help with the manuscript. And my greatest appreciation goes to my editor, Betsy Holt, who continues to teach me how to communicate beyond photographs.

These are two people who I cannot thank enough for their continuing efforts on my behalf: Lynnette Mager, my studio manager, who coordinated the project through months of shooting and post-production. And Dave Phillips, my digital artist, who has worked with me for years and in that time has helped create all the imagery pictured here. My sincerest thanks goes to them for their tireless efforts, talents, and support.

Tehabi Books developed, designed, and produced *Automobiles of the Chrome Age* and has conceived and produced many award-winning books that are recognized for their strong literary and visual content. Tehabi works with national and international publishers, corporations, institutions, and non-profit groups to identify, develop, and implement comprehensive publishing programs. Tehabi Books is located in San Diego, California. *www.tehabi.com*

President and Publisher Chris Capen
Senior Vice President Sam Lewis
Vice President and Creative Director Karla Olson
Director, Corporate Publishing Chris Brimble
Senior Art Director Josie Delker
Production Artist Monika Stout
Editor Betsy Holt
Copy Editor Marco Pavia
Proofreader Patrick Vincent

© 2004 by Tehabi Books, Inc.

Tehabi Books offers special discounts for bulk purchases for sales promotions and use as premiums. Specific, large-quantity needs can be met with special editions, custom covers, and by repurposing existing materials. For more information, contact Andrew Arias, corporate sales manager, at Tehabi Books, 4920 Carroll Canyon Road, Suite 200, San Diego, California 92121-3735; or by telephone at 800-243-7259.

Photographer and author Michael Furman has been photographing cars for more than three decades. His portfolio includes an extensive range of automobiles, including one-of-a-kind prototypes, Grand Prix cars, coachbuilt classics and sports cars. A recognized expert in digital capture and computer-generated imagery, he shoots cars exclusively in the studio, employing elegant lighting and classical design to showcase the personality of these wonderful machines. Michael can be reached at www.michaelfurman.com

All photographs copyright © 2004 Michael Furman

Editor Christopher Sweet
Editorial Assistant Sigi Nacson
Production Manager Kaija Markoe

Library of Congress Cataloging-in-Publication Data

Furman, Michael.
   Automobiles of the chrome age, 1946-1960 / Michael Furman.
      p. cm.
   "A Tehabi Book."
   Includes bibliographical references and index.
   ISBN 0-8109-4972-5 (hardcover)
   1. Automobiles--United States--History--20th century. I. Title.

   TL23.F87 2004
   629.222'0973'09045--dc22

                                    2004012637

Published in 2004 by Harry N. Abrams, Incorporated, New York.
All rights reserved. No part of the contents of this book may be reproduced without written permission of the publisher.

Printed and bound in Italy

10 9 8 7 6 5 4 3 2 1

Harry N. Abrams, Inc.
100 Fifth Avenue
New York, N.Y. 10011
www.abramsbooks.com

Abrams is a subsidiary of

LA MARTINIÈRE

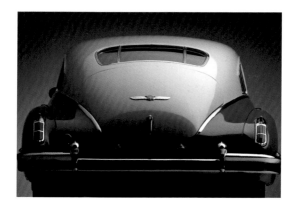